Bread from Heaven

Bread from Heaven

Prophetic Affirmations

BARBARA LYONS SLADE

To order additional copies of this book, contact:
Xlibris
844-714-8691
www.Xlibris.com
Orders@Xlibris.com
825231

Contents

Acknowledgements ix
What Are Prophetic Affirmations? xi
"My Story" xiii

1   Acknowledge God.. 1
2   An Atmosphere for Change 5
3   Before the Last Bite..9
4   Candy Corn Crave 13
5   Comfort Eating 17
6   Count the Cost...21
7   Daniel's Diet 25
8   Divine Warnings...29
9   Failing Forward..33
10   Finally Free 37
11   Fried Chicken & Biscuits 41
12   Fuel or Foolishness 45
13   Giants in the Land 49
14   God Is Enough 53
15   God Is on Our Side..57
16   God Satisfies the Soul..61
17   Honor Your Body...65
18   Icing on the Cake...69
19   Idols of the Heart..73
20   Is Anyone Thirsty? 77
21   It Matters...81
22   Just Do It...85
23   Let This Be the Day...89

24 Mindless Mornings...93
25 Never-Ending Temptations 97
26 Nicole's Story 101
27 No Greater Love 105
28 No Temptation Too Great...109
29 Not Without God.. 113
30 One Step at a Time... 117
31 Persevere in the Process.. 121
32 Plan to Prosper..125
33 Put God First 129
34 Ready or Not...133
35 Run Your Race...137
36 Say What You Pray 141
37 Speak the Word..145
38 Spiritual Menu...149
39 Stand for Something..153
40 Stop, Look & Listen 157
41 Stop Self-Sabotage... 161
42 The Battle Is Real 165
43 The Inner You 169
44 The Path of Success 173
45 Today Is Tomorrow...177
46 Use Your Voice 181
47 Watch Your Walk..185
48 What Are You Thinking? 189
49 Words of Life 193
50 Your Best Life 197

Acknowledgements

My sincere appreciation to my friend, Trudy Graves.
Thank you for your labor of love and your constant support.
You are my editing queen!

My deepest gratitude to my friend and photographer, Ruth Dudas.
Thank you for sharing your God-given gift.
You are truly a blessing to me.

And to my heavenly Father, to whom I owe everything.
Thank You for calling me to be Yours and for teaching
me how to change my life by what I say.

What Are Prophetic Affirmations?

Prophetic Affirmations are statements you make that align with the scriptures. They are words that you speak to keep yourself focused on what is right and true. They also help you to see yourself from God's perspective and equip you to do the things you were born to do.

Prophetic Affirmations are a gateway to change. They help you to overcome self-sabotaging thoughts so that you can make positive, purposeful changes to your life. The words you speak can reshape the narrative of your internal dialogue, create new beliefs, and boost your self-esteem.

Prophetic Affirmations are excellent tools to help you embrace the truth. When you affirm yourself with words that agree with God's will, it increases your faith and deepens your spiritual walk. The beauty of speaking words that correspond with the scriptures is that it helps you to achieve a reality that is God approved.

Prophetic Affirmations are a gift from God. Use them consistently and experience victory over your struggles and strength in areas of weakness. Speak about your potential and squash any negative thoughts that diminish your self-worth. Remind yourself often that God loves you, accepts you, and wants the best for you. Say what God says and affirm yourself in truth.

"My Story"

I used to say that my headstone would read "she died trying." I said that because I spent years talking about improving my eating habits but not putting in the work to change. I desired it, prayed for it, made many goals to attain it, but never stayed on course long enough to make a lifestyle change. There was a time I did not think I would do it at all.

I was an emotional eater. I ate mindlessly, and I ate because I could. Sitting down eating a big meal did not move me, nor did I enjoy talking about food. I just wanted what I wanted and then to eat it in private. Oh, I forgot to mention, I was a closet eater.

Food became my companion in happy times, during moments of frustration or disappointment, when I was anxious, bored, tired, or sleepy. Food was a faithful partner for all emotions, and eating was my crutch to cope with unwanted feelings. Additionally, for years, I suffered from chronic pain, and junk food was my drug of choice.

Nevertheless, God had a plan for me, which was to eat only enough to sustain myself and to speak Prophetic Affirmations to achieve it. It sounded easy. It did not take a lot of time or energy. There was no fee involved, no particular place required, and the rewards were beyond measure. All I had to do was to speak God's Word and empower myself to change. But, if I did that, and was successful, then I would have to give up eating what and how I wanted. So, I chose to keep eating.

I wrote several Prophetic Affirmations books and taught others how to affirm themselves with truth. But not until after I was diagnosed with cancer, prediabetes, and hypertension, did I ask myself, "How much longer are you willing to subject your body to sickness and disease? How much longer are you going to disobey God?" It was then that I decided to quit playing with my life and obey the word God had given me two decades before, which was from 1 Corinthians 9:27 NKJV "I discipline my body and bring it into subjection, lest, when I have preached to others, I myself should become disqualified."

God is faithful, and He never gave up on me. He encouraged me, admonished me, and strengthened me to persevere. And while I have not acquired perfection in my eating habits, I am stronger, wiser, more disciplined, and well on my way to a healthier lifestyle. I feel better, more in control, and, most importantly, I know God is pleased with my efforts. I also believe that my journey, with its many struggles and setbacks, was not in vain. The world is full of people who live in guilt, discouragement, and even shame because of how they eat. My story is a testimony that you can change your life by what you say. You can create new habits by the words of your mouth, and you can live your best life when you trust the one who gave you life. God is in the details, and "yes" He cares about what we eat.

It is my prayer that if you are battling the spirit of gluttony, caught in the vicious cycle of emotional eating, or enslaved to food on any level, that this book will be a catalyst to your freedom. I hope that my experiences and those of others mentioned in this work inspire you to use your voice to create the reality you want to see.

Embrace the possibility of being who God created you to be by what you say. Envision reaching goals that seem unattainable. Be in one accord with God's thoughts about you. Speak words that give you hope and strength and use your voice to empower yourself to succeed.

Thank God for the victory He has given us through His Word! "Death and life are in the power of the tongue" (Proverbs 18:21 NKJV).

Bread From Heaven

He knows about everyone, everywhere.
Everything about us is bare and wide open
to the all-seeing eyes of our living God;
nothing can be hidden from him to whom
we must explain all that we have done.
Hebrews 4:13 TLB

1

Acknowledge God

Hebrews 4:13 TLB tells us that God knows about everyone, everywhere, so there is nothing about us that escapes Him. He knows that we are weak, vulnerable to temptation, and drawn away by our own desires. God is familiar with our cravings and what triggers us to eat mindlessly. He knows all the reasons we eat outside of hunger pangs, and He knows when we have stumbled so often that a healthy lifestyle seems out of reach.

The Eternal God, who is all-knowing, all-powerful, and all-sufficient, cares about what we put in our bodies, and He is more than able to give us everything we need to develop and maintain good eating habits. Our heavenly Father will always help us, but He will not do it for us. We must actively participate in the process. The food is not going to disappear from our plates miraculously, nor can we expect someone to come along and push us away from the table. Every day we have to make a conscious decision to do what is best for our bodies, and if we trust God to help us stay on track, we will eventually achieve a healthier lifestyle.

Acknowledge God, and let the one who knows about everything that can be known, show you the reasons you overeat. Acknowledge God, and let the one who holds all power and might in His hands, empower you to make right decisions and walk away from those things that hinder your health. Acknowledge God, and let the one who created the heavens and the earth, the mountains and the seas, help you to honor your body and glorify Him in all that you do.

*In all your ways know and acknowledge
and recognize Him, and He will make your
paths straight and smooth [removing
obstacles that block your way].
Proverbs 3:6 AMP*

Prophetic Affirmations

I acknowledge God as the one who knows all things
I acknowledge God by submitting my will to His
I acknowledge God by trusting Him to help me
I acknowledge God in all my ways

*Speak the affirmations again.
Be inspired by what you say.*

I acknowledge God as the one who knows all things
I acknowledge God by submitting my will to His
I acknowledge God by trusting Him to help me
I acknowledge God in all my ways

I acknowledge God as the one who knows all things
I acknowledge God by submitting my will to His
I acknowledge God by trusting Him to help me
I acknowledge God in all my ways

Prayer for Today

Heavenly Father,
You are all-knowing and all-powerful.
You are the Lord God Almighty.
You alone are worthy of my praise.

Heavenly Father,
You know me best.
You are familiar with all my ways.
I acknowledge You, and I trust You.

Thank You for helping me to do
what honors You the most.
Thank You for caring about my life.
Thank You for caring about me.
In Jesus' name

Words are powerful; take them seriously.
Matthew 12:36 MSG

God merely spoke,
and the heavens were formed
and all the galaxies of stars.
Psalm 33:6 TLB

2

An Atmosphere for Change

For a long time, I had a "hit and miss" routine in speaking prophetic affirmations. I would periodically say them in the morning, during my fellowship with God, or with a friend. But saying them in the morning before any temptations arose was not enough to make a significant impact in the way I ate. I had to speak affirmations consistently, not only in the sweet moments with God or fellowship with friends but in the midst of temptation and when there was no temptation. I had to declare them morning and night until my words created the change I needed and desired.

I encourage you to start your day by reminding yourself how much God loves you and desires the best for you. Look up scriptures that talk about the blessings we receive as children of God and say those things. While dressing, speak words that honor your body and build your self-esteem. During the day rehearse words that will help you control your appetite and keep you focused on healthy living. Before you go to bed, find something inspiring to say to yourself.

You do not have to use a barrage of words to affirm yourself. Say what is sufficient for your situation. The main thing is to keep speaking until you believe what you say and do what you hear.

There is power in God's Word, and there is power in the words you speak. Therefore, saturate your mind with truth, lift your spirit with words that align with the scriptures, and say only those things that encourage, empower, and give you hope.

Kind words are like honey—
sweet to the soul and healthy for the body.
Proverbs 16:24 NLT

Prophetic Affirmations

I speak words that encourage my soul
I speak words that are healthy for my body
I speak words that lift my spirit
I speak words that create an atmosphere for change

I speak words that encourage my soul
I speak words that are healthy for my body
I speak words that lift my spirit
I speak words that create an atmosphere for change

What you say will make a difference.
What you say will change your life.

I speak words that encourage my soul
I speak words that are healthy for my body
I speak words that lift my spirit
I speak words that create an atmosphere for change

Prayer for Today

Holy God,
You spoke and created the heavens.
You breathed Your Word, and the world began.

Thank You for helping me to understand that
the words I speak have tremendous power.
The words I speak will help me to gain
control over my eating habits.
The words I speak will change my life.

Holy God,
May I always speak words that
encourage, strengthen, and give me hope.
In Jesus' name

Dear brothers and sisters,
never get tired of doing good.
2 Thessalonians 3:13 NLT

For we all stumble in many ways.
James 3:2 NIV

But thanks be to God!
He gives us the victory through
our Lord Jesus Christ.
1 Corinthians 15:57 NIV

3

Before the Last Bite

Have you ever wondered why we wait until we finish the last bite of something that we may say "that was not worth it, it was not that good, or why did I eat it?" Or how about when we assess the nutritional facts of some non-essential food after we have consumed it.

Human nature is baffling. We usually think about doing the right thing after we have indulged in wrongdoing. We want to do what we know we should but often end up doing the opposite. As the Apostle Paul so aptly expressed in Romans 7:19 TLB, "When I want to do good, I don't; and when I try not to do wrong, I do it anyway."

Emotional or physical trauma can trigger eating without thought. The inability to read or comprehend nutritional facts can also play a part in poor eating habits. But, generally, we opt for instant gratification when we should be thinking about what we are ingesting and the effect it has on our health.

Maybe you have found yourself eating as if on autopilot, and not until after that last bite did you ask yourself, "why am I eating? Instead, you probably felt disappointed, realizing that once again, you chose to eat without counting the cost.

You are not alone, and you are not hopeless. We all stumble until we get it right. You may do the very thing you do not want to do the next time or the time after that. But if you stay focused on your health and consistent with your efforts, you will eventually make the right choice and do what is best for your body before the last bite.

For if your life is just about satisfying the impulses of your sinful nature, then prepare to die. But if you have invited the Spirit to destroy these selfish desires, you will experience life.
Romans 8:13 VOICE

I will not die; instead, I will live to tell what the Lord has done.
Psalm 118:17 NLT

Prophetic Affirmations

I will make wise decisions
I will invest in my health
I will change the way I eat
I will live and not die

Repeat the affirmations.
Be empowered by what you hear.

I will make wise decisions
I will invest in my health
I will change the way I eat
I will live and not die

Prayer for Today

Mighty God,
You are all-powerful.
You are the ruler of the world.
There is no one above You.

Thank You for giving me the resolve
to do what is best for my body.
Thank You for helping me to stay
focused on my health.

I believe I can change the way I eat, and
I believe I can do all things in Christ.
In Jesus' name, I pray

*For the world offers only a craving
for physical pleasure, a craving for everything
we see, and pride in our achievements
and possessions. These are not from the
Father, but are from this world.*
1 John 2:16 NLT

4

Candy Corn Crave

Did you know that 22 pieces of candy corn contain 28 grams of sugar, and if you ate an 11-ounce bag of these little bombs, it would be the same as eating 18 tablespoons of white sugar?

Well, a dear friend of mine did consume a bag of candy corn and not just once, but many times over, and each time she indulged, she ate herself senseless. Everyone at her workplace knew she loved them. So, during October, when you find candy corn on every store shelf in anticipation of Halloween, my friend received several bags. She would store them neatly in her file drawer and eat a few pieces at a time. As she reached for more, repeatedly without thought, she devoured an entire bag before the day was over.

Imagine the cataclysmic effect all that sugar had on her body. Her heart was beating faster than usual, her stomach was queasy, and she felt like she wanted to gag. She experienced brain fog, blurred vision, lacked concentration, and sometimes fell asleep at her desk.

We jeopardize our health because of too much sugar in our diet, even when we know sugar wreaks havoc on our organs and makes us susceptible to sickness and disease. So why do we subject ourselves to such detriment? Why do we choose to shorten our lives? While we may not know what compels us to indulge in harmful habits, God, who knows our innermost thoughts, is ready and willing to show us the reasons behind our actions, strengthen us to change, and deliver us from cravings that do us no good.

When you're given a box of candy, don't
gulp it all down; eat too much chocolate
and you'll make yourself sick.
Proverbs 25:16 MSG

Prophetic Affirmations

I will eat in moderation
I will exercise self-control
I will do what it takes to promote my health

Speak the affirmations again.
Concentrate on the words as you say them.

I will eat in moderation
I will exercise self-control
I will do what it takes to promote my health

Speak the affirmations once more.
Speak them until you do what you say.

I will eat in moderation
I will exercise self-control
I will do what it takes to promote my health

Prayer for Today

Heavenly Father,
Lord God Almighty,
You are my God.
I honor Your holy name.

Forgive me for the times I chose to overindulge
even when I knew I was harming myself.
Forgive me for dishonoring my body.
Please help me to stop eating foolishly.
You are my only hope.
To You alone, I pray.
In Jesus' name

Let My perfect peace calm you in every circumstance and give you courage and strength for every challenge.
John 14:27 AMP

He commanded the storm to calm down, and it became still. A hush came over the waves of the sea.
Psalm 107:29 VOICE

5

Comfort Eating

Many of us attempt to use food as a diversion from pain, a coping mechanism, or a source of comfort. Many of us also find ourselves dominated by food addictions, eating disorders, lack of restraint, and poor decision-making when it comes to what we put in our bodies.

Eating something tasty, especially foods high in sugar or foods that invoke pleasant memories, may often produce momentary feelings of contentment. I cannot deny that I have personally tried to take the edge off some emotional annoyance with cookies, a bowl of ice cream, a bag of chips, or whatever was at hand. I have also discovered that comfort eating is a false fix and deprives you of the opportunity to deal with your feelings in a healthy manner.

Try to remember how you felt the last time you ate to comfort yourself. After you savored that last bite of food, were you no longer bored? Did your frustration subside? Did eating calm your angry feelings or diminish your stress in any significant way?

Most likely, it did not. So, I encourage you to give yourself the freedom to feel what you feel and do not try to suppress your emotions with food. Take time to do some quiet introspection. Yield yourself to the Lord. Let your heavenly Father touch your heart and soothe your soul. Your feelings will not catch God off guard for He knows everything about us and waits for us to trust in His faithfulness. He is our heavenly Father and the source of all comfort, and even if food would calm you for a moment, God's comforting presence is for all times.

I was very worried and upset, but you
comforted me and made me happy!
Psalm 94:19 ERV

Prophetic Affirmations

God is my comforter
God is the one who calms my heart
God is the one who soothes my soul
God is the one who makes me happy

<u>Declare the Word over and over</u>
<u>and let the truth comfort you.</u>

God is my comforter
God is the one who calms my heart
God is the one who soothes my soul
God is the one who makes me happy

God is my comforter
God is the one who calms my heart
God is the one who soothes my soul
God is the one who makes me happy

Prayer for Today

Heavenly Father,
You are a mighty comforter, and I know
You can calm the storms in my life
just as you calmed the waves of the sea.

Heavenly Father,
Your compassion and tender mercies
surpass anything this world has to offer.

Forgive me for the times I chose food as a
source of comfort instead of coming to You.
Please help me to process my feelings in a
healthy way and to surrender my heart, my
thoughts, and all my concerns to You.
In Jesus' name, I pray

Heed (pay attention to)
instruction and be wise, and
do not ignore or neglect it.
Proverbs 8:33 AMP

Take hold of instruction; do not let
go. Guard her, for she is your life.
Proverbs 4:13 ESV

6

Count the Cost

Some time ago, my aunt had a traumatic experience after eating some homemade Thai food. The recipe called for two kinds of fish sauces, which were both high in sodium. However, my aunt ignored the recipe's recommended amount of sauce and prepared the dish according to her taste. In the end, she used approximately two cups of sauce, which is roughly 16,000 mg of sodium (keep in mind a healthy amount of sodium per day is 1,500-2,300 mg). Fully satisfied after eating this meal, my aunt settled in for the night and fell asleep. A few hours later, the pounding of her heart awakened her, which led to an emergency dispatch call. The paramedics came out, stabilized her vitals, and recommended she follow up with her doctor.

The next day my aunt went to see her doctor. He told her that the high sodium caused an imbalance in her electrolytes, which changed the rhythm of her heartbeat, and he scheduled her for further tests. After the initial exam, she went back home (still in a delicate state) and proceeded to eat more of the Thai dish.

I know it sounds utterly foolish that she would put herself in such a precarious position, but let us not be so quick to judge, for how often have we eaten something we knew was harmful, even to the point of discomfort or sickness, but continued to do it anyway.

I urge you to count the cost and pay attention to what you put in your bódy. Nothing is worth jeopardizing your health. Nothing is worth forfeiting your future. Nothing is worth being out of God's will.

Tune your ears to wisdom, and
concentrate on understanding.
Proverbs 2:2 NLT

Prophetic Affirmations

I tune my ears to wisdom
I concentrate on understanding
I count the cost before I eat

Repeat the affirmations.
Listen to the words as you speak.

I tune my ears to wisdom
I concentrate on understanding
I count the cost before I eat

Speak the words again.
Be changed by what you say.

I tune my ears to wisdom
I concentrate on understanding
I count the cost before I eat

Prayer for Today

Father of all Grace,
You are mighty and awesome,
perfect in all Your ways, and yet You accept
me and love me with all my imperfections.

Forgive me for the times I treated my body
poorly and dishonored the gift of my life.

Please help me to make wise choices,
pay attention to what I eat, and honor
my body that I may honor You.
In Jesus' name, I pray

When you go out to dinner with an influential
person, mind your manners: Don't gobble your
food, don't talk with your mouth full. And don't
stuff yourself, bridle your appetite.
Proverbs 23:2-3 MSG

You're blessed when you've worked up a
good appetite for God. He's food and drink
in the best meal you'll ever eat.
Matthew 5:6 MSG

7

Daniel's Diet

Daniel had the opportunity to eat some of the most exceptional food in the land. Meals prepared for the king - savory meats, fresh loaves of bread, delicious desserts, and delicacies of all sorts. I am sure it was something to see, as well as partake. However, Daniel resolved not to eat the food from the royal table. Instead, he asked the attendant to test him and his three friends for ten days by giving them a diet of pulse (seeds and grains) and water. At the end of the ten days, Daniel and his friends looked healthier and better nourished than the young men who had been eating the food assigned by the king. (Daniel 1)

There are many occasions and a host of social events that present opportunities for us to indulge in gourmet meals, holiday dishes, mouthwatering appetizers, and homemade desserts. These are also the times to exercise self-control over our eating habits and to consider the cost of what we eat before we put it in our bodies. Healthy eating does not mean we have to eat pulse as Daniel and his friends did. We can enjoy a delicious cuisine or some tasty treats from time to time. The important thing is that we manage our health and not let fleshly desires drive us to overeat just because the opportunity exists.

Decide to do what is best for your body before the temptations arise and settle in your heart to honor God by glorifying Him in whatever you do. By doing so, you will have a ready answer for every occasion, and the more you surrender to this way of living, the stronger you will become spiritually, mentally, and physically.

Whether you eat or drink, or whatever
you do, do it all for the glory of God.
1 Corinthians 10:31 NLT

Prophetic Affirmations

I manage my health
I exercise self-control
I take care of my body
I live my life to glorify God

I manage my health
I exercise self-control
I take care of my body
I live my life to glorify God

Repeat the affirmations until you can say them with
your eyes closed. Then take a moment and visualize
yourself standing before a table full of tempting and
delicious foods. Say the affirmations once more and
imagine the choices you would make if you
were eating "to glorify God."

Prayer for Today

Great and glorious God,
You are full of splendor and majesty.
I bless Your holy name.

Great and glorious God,
You alone created the universe.
You reign from the highest heavens.
You are sovereign over all things.
I bless Your holy name.

Great and glorious God,
You are mighty in all Your works.
You are perfect in all Your ways.
There is none like You, Lord.
I praise You now and forever!
In Jesus' name

*And if you leave God's paths and go
astray, you will hear a voice behind you
say, "No, this is the way; walk here."*
Isaiah 30:21 TLB

*Let us follow the Holy Spirit's
leading in every part of our lives.*
Galatians 5:25 TLB

8

Divine Warnings

One day my sister offered me some Popeye's Chicken, but as I thought about the grease going through my body and the regret I would feel after I ate it, I refused the offer. A couple of days later, she went to Popeye's again and offered to get me a meal, and this time, I chose to accept. I could only eat a couple of bites of the chicken because the little pieces of fat underneath the thick layer of fried skin looked gross. Additionally, the gravy on the mashed potatoes was oily. I should have thrown them in the trash. Instead, I quickly mixed the gravy in the potatoes to hide the oil and proceeded to eat. Three hours later, my stomach started gurgling and cramping, and for the next several days, I suffered from what I believe was food poisoning.

In hindsight, the feeling that I had the first time I refused Popeye's was a warning from the Holy Spirit. God knew what was going to happen, and I paid a dear price for not yielding to His voice.

Here is what I gleaned from the experience: 1) The Holy Spirit's warning did not change from one day to the next. 2) I did not pass the test of hearing and obeying God. 3) In my physical distress, I vowed to God that I would never eat at Popeye's again, which should have been my attitude when I received His initial warning. 4) My one wrong choice resulted in a relatively mild case of food poisoning, but consistent disobedience to God is disastrous to our well-being and our life in general. Lastly, was the reminder that God is in the details. All we need to do is listen and obey.

Those who trust their own insight are foolish,
but anyone who walks in wisdom is safe.
Proverbs 28:26 NLT

Prophetic Affirmations

I walk in wisdom
I listen to God's voice
I obey what God tells me to do
I walk in wisdom, and I am safe

I am safe because I walk in wisdom
I am safe because I listen to God's voice
I am safe because I obey the Lord

Empower yourself by what you say.
Empower yourself to do what God tells you to do.

I walk in wisdom
I listen to God's voice
I obey what God tells me to do
I walk in wisdom, and I am safe

Prayer for Today

Holy God,
You called me out of the world to be Yours.
You adopted me into Your family.
You gave me Your Spirit.
You opened my ears to hear from You.
You gave me the ability to discern Your voice.

Holy God,
Forgive me for the times I ignored You.
I repent for the times I did not obey.
Help me to do better, Lord.
Help me to do what You say.
In Jesus' name, I pray

No, dear brothers and sisters, I have not
achieved it, but I focus on this one thing:
Forgetting the past and looking forward to what
lies ahead, I press on to reach the end of the race
and receive the heavenly prize for which God,
through Christ Jesus, is calling us.
Philippians 3:13-14 NLT

9

Failing Forward

Even in our best attempt to eat healthier, we will, at times, make wrong food choices, overeat, or eat too late at night. We may not stay within our desired eating plan. Our calorie consumption may go over what we intend. There may even be times when we use food to soothe an emotional void or to alleviate stress.

Rest assured that these are not the times to beat yourself up or allow anyone else to make light of your efforts to improve your health. Stand firm in your desire to do right because your adversary, the devil, is waiting to destroy your self-esteem and steal your hope for success. Stay on guard and give him no room to muddle your mind or cause you to have a defeatist attitude.

If you fail to make a healthy choice, but it helps you to identify your eating triggers, you have failed forward. If you fail to stay within your eating plan, but it makes you more determined to do better the next time, you have failed forward. Each time you make a mistake, and you get up and try again, you have failed forward.

Everyone fails sometimes, but winners keep their eyes on the goal, and they never quit. Look at an athlete who may fall short of the prize many times, but he does not give up on his dream. He keeps training, competing, and believing that one day, he will hold the championship trophy. In the same way, never abandon your efforts to eat healthier. If you fall, get up. If you stumble, brush yourself off. Keep failing forward, stay focused, and never give up!

I have fought the good fight, I have
finished the race, I have kept the faith.
2 Timothy 4:7 NKJV

Prophetic Affirmations

I run my race with faith
I stay focused on the goal
I keep going no matter what happens
I fight to finish strong

Speak the words over and over.
Boost your confidence by what you say.
Repetition is the key!

I run my race with faith
I stay focused on the goal
I keep going no matter what happens
I fight to finish strong

I run my race with faith
I stay focused on the goal
I keep going no matter what happens
I fight to finish strong

Prayer for Today

Heavenly Father,
Your faithfulness is eternal.
Your kindness is everlasting.

Thank You for never giving up
on me and for giving me the strength
to not give up on myself.

Help me to run my race with faith and to see
myself as the winner You created me to be.
With You on my side, I cannot fail.

Thank You for all that You do for me.
My life is in Your hands.
To You alone, I pray.
In Jesus' name

We have freedom now, because Christ made
us free. So stand strong in that freedom.
Don't go back into slavery again.
Galatians 5:1 ERV

You were called to be free. But do
not let this freedom become an excuse for
letting your physical desires control you.
Galatians 5:13 GNT

10

Finally Free

I remember a time when I ate sweets several times a day, every day. The more I ingested, the more I wanted. I would start my day off by purchasing a pastry or candy bar from the vending machine at work. Once I had that first fix, I was ready for more. A half an hour later I would pay another visit to the vending machine, this time hiding my goods in the sleeve of my blouse, pockets of my sweater, or between office files. At lunchtime, I made my way to the local bakery, where I happily bought a selection of treats. In the evening I went back to the bakery or some nearby store. In between my regular supply of sugar, I made a routine stop to anyone who kept candy or other choice items on their desk. Filled with guilt, I prayed every night to be free of this behavior, and though I prayed for help, I felt like I should have been able to change my ways on my own, after all, it was only food.

On June 8, 1991, God delivered me from sugar addiction, and though I was more in control of my eating than ever before, it was not until years later that I walked in the liberty He had given me that day. I thank God for hearing my cry for help.

Nothing is too hard for God. He can deliver us from everything that has us bound, no matter how bad it seems. Choose to be free from food addiction and bad eating habits. Ask God to help you and expect Him to do a miracle in your life, so that one day, like myself, you will be able to say with conviction and confidence, "Food has no control over me, and I am living my life finally free."

So if the Son sets you free, you are truly free.
John 8:36 NLT

Prophetic Affirmations

I am free to eat healthy
Food has no control over me
I am free to eat healthy
I am truly free

*Remind yourself daily of the liberty you have
in Christ. Speak about it. Declare it. Rehearse it.*

I am free to eat healthy
Food has no control over me
I am free to eat healthy
I am truly free

Keep talking until you believe what you say.

I am free to eat healthy
Food has no control over me
I am free to eat healthy
I am truly free

Prayer for Today

Dear Lord,
You are the Most High God.
You are the Everlasting Father.
You are the only living God.
I worship Your holy name.

You are my deliverer.
You are my redeemer.
You are my hope.
You are my strength.
Thank You for setting me free
and for giving me the victory.
In Jesus' name

Let the Holy Spirit guide your lives. Then you won't be doing what your sinful nature craves. The sinful nature wants to do evil, which is just the opposite of what the Spirit wants. And the Spirit gives us desires that are the opposite of what the sinful nature desires. These two forces are constantly fighting each other, so you are not free to carry out your good intentions.
Galatians 5:16-17 NLT

11

Fried Chicken & Biscuits

Fried chicken and biscuits may call your name.
White chocolate and cheesecake may do the same.
You can say "no" and resist the sound of their snare.
But not without God's Spirit, His Word, and much prayer.

A variety of cookies, crackers, and chips,
Beckon from the store aisles, tempting you to slip.
You can walk away victoriously and leave them on the shelf,
If you speak the Word of God and empower yourself.

Special luncheons, parties, events of all kinds,
Will even threaten a "made-up" mind.
Resolve to stand firm and do not fall for every treat.
Master self-restraint and let wisdom dictate what you eat.

Your carnal nature will never lead you to do as you should.
Depend upon the Holy Spirit to show you what is good.
And watch out for the devil who seeks to destroy.
Yes, even fried chicken and biscuits can be a ploy.

Practice self-control and do all things in moderation.
Rest assured the Sovereign Lord will give you strength
for every temptation.

Be sober [well balanced and self-disciplined],
be alert and cautious at all times. The enemy of
yours, the devil, prowls around like a roaring lion
[fiercely hungry), seeking someone to devour.
1 Peter 5:8 AMP

Prophetic Affirmations

I am well balanced
I am self-disciplined
I am alert
I am cautious at all times

Repeat the affirmations.
There is power in what you say.

I am well balanced
I am self-disciplined
I am alert
I am cautious at all times

I am well balanced
I am self-disciplined
I am alert
I am cautious at all times

Prayer for Today

Lord of Heaven,
You reign over all that exists.
You hold all power in Your hand.
Holy is Your name.

Lord of Heaven,
You have given me strength
for every temptation.
You have caused me to
triumph over my enemies.
You have given me victory in
every area of my life.
You are all that I need,
and I worship You.
In Jesus' name

Leave behind your foolishness and begin to live.
Proverbs 9:6 TLB

Learn to be wise and develop good judgment
and common sense! Cling to wisdom—she will
protect you. Love her—she will guard you.
Getting wisdom is the most important thing
you can do! And with your wisdom, develop
common sense and good judgment.
Proverbs 4:5-7 TLB

12

Fuel or Foolishness

It is foolish to eat until your stomach hurts. It does not make sense to keep putting food in your mouth until you feel so stuffed that you can hardly move, your brain is foggy, physical energy is low, and all you can do is wait in misery until you have digested the food.

It is also foolish to use food as a means to appease emotional needs. Food is fuel for the physical body. We need it to survive, and we should eat when we are hungry. But food does not solve boredom, nor is it the answer to anxiety or fear. Food is not a companion for loneliness, and it does not take away anger or frustration. And here is a real newsflash! Eating does not eliminate stress.

A delicious dessert may be a soothing placebo, but sugar and flour will never heal a wounded heart. Dining for days will help pass the time, but nothing cures boredom like a platter of purpose and inspiration. There are many things we can do to curb an angry spirit, but eating until we cannot see straight is not one of them.

Overeating offers no benefits, and using food as a means to soothe emotions is superficial. However, many of us will still try to "fix our feelings" with something we put in our belly. We may even think "I have to do something to cope, and at least eating is not as bad as doing drugs or drinking." Do not be foolish! Overeating may not distort your reasoning, but it is detrimental to your physical and mental well-being. For this reason, learn to manage your emotions, choose to eat wisely, and do everything you can to prolong your life.

*You were told that your foolish desires will
destroy you and that you must give up your
old way of life with all its bad habits.
Ephesians 4:22 CEV*

*Now your attitudes and thoughts must all
be constantly changing for the better.
Ephesians 4:23 TLB*

Prophetic Affirmations

I give up foolish desires
My attitude is changing

I give up my old way of life
My thoughts are changing

I give up bad eating habits
My life is changing

*Keep speaking the Word. Keep hearing
the Word. It will change your thoughts. It will
change your attitude. It will change your life!*

Prayer for Today

Heavenly Father,
You are above all and before all.
You are the First and the Last,
the Beginning and the End.
All power is in Your hands.

Heavenly Father,
I do not know why eating healthy is such a
struggle for me, or why I choose to allow
food to be a companion for my emotions,
but I know with Your help, I can change.

Thank You for never abandoning me.
Thank You for the victory I have in You.
Thank You for everything You do for me.
In Jesus' name, I pray

The Lord said to Moses, "Send some men to explore the land of Canaan, which I am giving to the Israelites."
Numbers 13:1-2 NIV

"For I know the plans I have for you," declares the Lord, "plans to prosper you and not to harm you, plans to give you hope and a future."
Jeremiah 29:11 NIV

13

Giants in the Land

The Bible tells us that twelve men went to Canaan and explored it for forty days. Two of the men came back, believing they could possess the land. The other ten came back with this report: "We entered the land you sent us to explore, and it is indeed a bountiful country - a land flowing with milk and honey. But the people living there are powerful. We even saw giants. We can't go up against them! They are stronger than we are!" (Numbers 13:27-31 NLT)

Many people fear what they perceive as too big to overcome, like the men who feared what they saw in the land of Canaan. They could have prevailed over the giants, just as we can overcome bad habits, but when we allow fear and doubt to distract us from our purpose, we forfeit all kinds of blessings and opportunities.

It takes real introspection to identify your fears, and it takes the power of God, working in you, to conquer them. I encourage you to ask yourself, "What do I fear? What is keeping me from receiving God's best?" Be prayerful as the answers to these questions and more come before you. Your fears may seem giant-size, even paralyzing, but the more you trust God, the less fear will dominate you.

Two of the twelve men believed they could possess the land of Canaan because they kept their eyes on God. Likewise, believe that God wants you to triumph over everything that prevents you from prospering in your health. God will help you to face your giants. The Lord of heaven and earth will help you to conquer your fears.

I prayed to the Lord, and he answered me.
He freed me from all my fears.
Psalm 34:4 NLT

For God has not given us a spirit of fear and
timidity, but of power, love, and self-discipline.
2 Timothy 1:7 NLT

Prophetic Affirmations

I can conquer my fears
I can face my giants
I can live a healthier life
I can possess all that God has for me

Speak the affirmations again.
Listen carefully to the words you say.
Strengthen your resolve by what you hear.

I can conquer my fears
I can face my giants
I can live a healthier life
I can possess all that God has for me

Prayer for Today

Heavenly Father,
You alone are God!
Only You are a mighty rock.
You give me strength and guide
me right. Your way is perfect and
Your Word is correct. You are a shield
for those who run to You for help.
Psalm 18:30-32 CEV

Thank You for helping me to face my giants.
Thank You for helping me to conquer my fears.
You are a mighty rock and your way is perfect.
Nothing is impossible with You.
In Jesus' name, I pray

Those who know you, Lord, will trust you;
you do not abandon anyone who comes to you.
Psalm 9:10 GNT

For that is what God is like.
He is our God forever and ever,
and he will guide us until we die.
Psalm 48:14 NLT

14

God Is Enough

There are times we may feel we cannot achieve a goal unless we have a partner, a mentor, or some support system. While there is nothing wrong with help (for we need counselors, doctors, dietary programs, and more, to help us conqueror poor eating habits), God wants us to trust Him. The Sovereign Lord, creator of the universe, knew us before we took one breath, and He understands the issues of our hearts. He knows how we handle the challenges of life, and He knows the deeper reasons we indulge in mindless and harmful habits.

God is enough, and He is an ever-present help. He is the almighty, self-sufficient God, who transcends all things and possesses all power. The Lord is all-wise and all-knowing, full of compassion and tender mercies. He is our deliverer, our hope, and our strength. In God, we have everything we need.

In those moments, when you feel that you need someone to help you eat more nutritionally, succeed in your weight loss efforts, and generally take better care of yourself, acknowledge God. He knows every battle you face and the temptations you endure, and He will give you everything you need to succeed. Sometimes that involves another person, a specific eating plan, maybe even a medical procedure. But it is only by the power of the living God and our willingness to "choose Him" over everything else that ultimately gives us the victory. There is no lack in God. He is enough. Trust in His faithfulness. He is the one who will keep you on track!

Trust God from the bottom of your heart; don't try to figure out everything on your own. Listen for God's voice in everything you do, everywhere you go; he's the one who will keep you on track.
Proverbs 3:5-6 MSG

Prophetic Affirmations

I listen for the Lord's voice in everything I do
God is the one who will keep me on track
God is the one I trust

I listen for the Lord's voice in everything I do
God is the one who will keep me on track
God is the one I trust

Speak the affirmations again. Pause after each sentence. There is power in God's Word. There is power in what you say.

I listen for the Lord's voice in everything I do
God is the one who will keep me on track
God is the one I trust

Prayer for Today

Father God,
You are the Lord God Almighty and
there is none greater than You.
You are my hope and my strength.
You are the one I trust.

Thank You for walking alongside me.
Thank You for keeping me on track.
Thank You for being my God.
You are more than enough for me.
In Jesus' name

But those who trust in the Lord for
help will find their strength renewed.
They will rise on wings like eagles;
they will run and not get weary;
they will walk and not grow weak.
Isaiah 40:31 GNT

15

God Is on Our Side

With God on our side, we can develop good eating habits. We can stop overindulging. We can control our appetites and make wiser food choices. We can lay aside junk food and find better ways to cope with emotional distress. We can stop eating mindlessly. We can resist temptation and stand firm against the works of darkness. We can live a healthier life and we can treat our bodies well.

With God on our side, we can do anything. With His Spirit working in us, we have the potential to rise above our struggles and prosper in everything we do. But human nature is inherently weak, and we will stumble, yield to temptation, lose our focus, and sometimes fall by the wayside. The good news is that God will never leave us nor give up on us. He will not criticize us nor make us feel guilty, regardless of our faults.

God knows that temptation comes from our own desires. He also knows the plans of wickedness set up against us and how cunningly the adversary works to detour us from living our best life. Regardless of what we face or how it comes, we can depend on God to help us. He is our safety net, our anchor, and the one in whom we can trust.

With God on our side, we can succeed. He is with us at all times, working in us and for us. As we surrender our will to God's will, we position ourselves for victory. In Christ, we cannot lose, and we cannot be defeated. The Everlasting God, maker of all that exists, loves us unconditionally, and He wants the best for us.

So, what do you think? With God on our
side like this, how can we lose?
Romans 8:31 MSG

Prophetic Affirmations

With God on my side, I can control my appetite
With God on my side, I can change the way I eat
With God on my side, I can do what I was born to do

Repeat the affirmations. Emphasize the words "I can."

With God on my side, I can control my appetite
With God on my side, I can change the way I eat
With God on my side, I can do what I was born to do

Repeat the affirmations once more.
Be empowered by the words of your mouth.

With God on my side, I can control my appetite
With God on my side, I can change the way I eat
With God on my side, I can do what I was born to do

Prayer for Today

Sovereign Lord,
You are a great God.
You are faithful in all Your ways.
I praise Your holy name.

Please help me to prosper in my
health, take care of my body, and
gain control over my appetite.
Help me to do what I know I should do.

Sovereign Lord,
You are mighty in all Your ways.
Please help me to honor You.
Help me to surrender my will to Yours.
In Jesus' name, I pray

The Lord will continually guide you, and
satisfy your soul in scorched and dry places,
and give strength to your bones; And you will
be like a watered garden, and like a spring of
water whose waters do not fail.
Isaiah 58:11 AMP

16

God Satisfies the Soul

If you habitually eat to suppress emotions, you must have noticed that after you have consumed the ice cream, cookies, cake, chips, or whatever your food indulgence consists of, that you are still looking for more. That is because sugar craves more sugar, carbs crave more carbs, and an unsettled soul desires to be satisfied.

I admit my first instinct was to head to the kitchen when I was trying to work through unwanted feelings. Cookies and popcorn had often proved to be a good distraction, but never has food clarified my thoughts, calmed my heart, or soothed the uneasiness in my soul. On the contrary, I felt more agitated because of the sugar high. My stomach was jittery because of the junk food I had ingested, and I felt flustered and foolish because I had not resolved anything.

Have you ever seen the words "this will guarantee less anxiety or take away frustration" on a bag of chips or a carton of ice cream? Probably not. But the Bible, which is absolute truth, tells us in Psalm 107:9 AMPC that "God satisfies the longing soul." Yes, our loving God will satisfy the soul that longs for comfort and peace.

When you feel agitated, frustrated, discouraged, or generally out of sorts, spend time with God. Choose Him, worship Him, and talk to Him, instead of looking for something to eat. Food is the solution to physical hunger; it is not the answer to emotional discomfort. Only God can calm your heart and ease your anxieties. Only God, who knows your deepest needs, can satisfy your soul.

For He satisfies the longing soul and
fills the hungry soul with good.
Psalm 107:9 AMPC

Prophetic Affirmations

I depend on God to ease my anxieties
I depend on God to calm my heart
I depend on God to satisfy my soul

Encourage yourself by the words of your mouth.

I depend on God to ease my anxieties
I depend on God to calm my heart
I depend on God to satisfy my soul

Increase your faith by what you say.
Be strengthened by what you hear.

I depend on God to ease my anxieties
I depend on God to calm my heart
I depend on God to satisfy my soul

Prayer for Today

Before the mountains were born,
before You gave birth to the earth and
the world, You were God. You are God
from everlasting to everlasting.
Psalm 90:2 GW

Thank You for Your lovingkindness.
Thank You for meeting my needs.
Thank You for easing my anxieties.
Thank You for satisfying my soul.
Thank You for being my God.
In Jesus' name

I look at your heavens, which you made with your fingers. I see the moon and stars, which you created. But why are people even important to you? Why do you take care of human beings? You made them a little lower than the angels and crowned them with glory and honor.
Psalm 8:3-5 NCV

17

Honor Your Body

The human body is composed of several systems that work intricately and simultaneously as one miraculous organism. Each system has a unique purpose and is dependent upon the others to work effectively. Within each system are major organs. Within each organ are different types of tissues with specific functions, and within the tissues are trillions of cells of various shapes and sizes.

The human body is far too complicated to describe here and while no one can fully understand all its complexities, Ephesians 2:10 tells us that we are God's handiwork, His masterpiece, and His workmanship. Genesis 2:7 NLT says that "God formed the man from the dust of the ground. He breathed the breath of life into the man's nostrils, and the man became a living person." In Psalm 139:13 NLT, David says "You made all the delicate, inner parts of my body and knit me together in my mother's womb," and in Psalm 100:3 NIV, it says, "Know that the Lord is God. It is He who made us, and we are His."

Since God created our bodies, who are we to break them down? Who are we to destroy His perfect work? Have we yet to understand that the body is a vessel of honor, a gift from God, and a gift to God, made for His glory and purpose?

Our response to God's gift of life should be to take care of our bodies so that we can become the extraordinary people He created us to be. Let us, therefore, honor God by honoring His handiwork. Let us honor God by honoring our bodies.

You alone created my inner being.
You knitted me together inside my mother.
I will give thanks to You because I have been
so amazingly and miraculously made.
Psalm 139:13-14 GW

Prophetic Affirmations

I am God's handiwork
I am wonderful and amazing
Everything about me is a miracle

Honor God by the words of your mouth.

I am God's handiwork
I am wonderful and amazing
Everything about me is a miracle

Honor God by what you say.

I am God's handiwork
I am wonderful and amazing
Everything about me is a miracle

Prayer for Today

Holy God,
You created every living thing.
You are my heavenly Father,
and I worship You.

Forgive me for subjecting my body to obesity,
and all kinds of conditions and discomforts.
I repent for not taking care of myself.
I repent for eating without restraint.

Please help me to love myself, and
to honor You with all that I do.
In Jesus' name

Keep watch and pray,
so that you will not give in to temptation.
For the spirit is willing, but the body is weak.
Mark 14:38 NLT

A person without self-control
is like a city with broken-down walls.
Proverbs 25:28 NLT

18

Icing on the Cake

I was watching television one afternoon, and a car commercial came on with the storyline of a woman rushing to get a cake to a birthday party. The precision and power of the car enabled the woman to maneuver through traffic and get to her destination on time, with the white iced cake still intact on the back seat.

A little later, a commercial came on for Xeljanz, which is a medication for rheumatoid arthritis. It showed a woman, who after taking Xeljanz for some time, was able to bake a white iced cake without experiencing any pain in her hands.

Shortly after that, a Food Network commercial came on advertising a competition for the best white cake with white icing. You can only imagine what I was thinking after seeing three commercials within an hour of each other that included white cake with white icing.

The commercials did not tempt me (or so I thought) even though cake is one of my favorite desserts. But a few days later I went to the store, and in robot style, I went straight to the bakery section and bought a big slice of white cake with white icing. In hindsight, I should have recognized the subtle temptation coming through the TV. Instead, I watched idly and fell into the trap of mindless eating.

My word of advice is to keep alert because whether it is a white iced cake, a sizzling burger, or perfectly fried chicken, there will always be a commercial, a billboard, or some other advertisement that appeals to your taste buds and entices you to come and partake.

Keep alert at all times.
Luke 21:36 NLT

Prophetic Affirmations

I keep alert at all times
I watch out for common pitfalls
I am quick to recognize subtle temptations
I pay attention to what I see

I keep alert at all times
I watch out for common pitfalls
I am quick to recognize subtle temptations
I pay attention to what I see

Repeat these words until they
resonate in your soul.
Repeat them until you do what you say.

I keep alert at all times
I watch out for common pitfalls
I am quick to recognize subtle temptations
I pay attention to what I see

Prayer for Today

Lord of Heaven,
You are the almighty God.
Holy is Your name.

Thank You for keeping me alert to the
pitfalls the enemy has set up against me.
Thank You for helping me to stand firm
against the desires of my flesh.

Lord of Heaven,
You are the all-powerful God.
Holy is Your name.

Thank You for helping me with my struggles.
Thank You for causing me to triumph.
In Jesus' name, I pray

Those who cling to worthless idols
turn away from God's love for them.
Jonah 2:8 NIV

The Lord God says:
"Repent and destroy your idols, and
stop worshiping them in your hearts."
Ezekiel 14:6 TLB

19

Idols of the Heart

One day I was slightly frustrated because I had to go somewhere that I did not want to go. To take the edge off my emotional displeasure, I immediately begin to search for something to eat. Since I had to go out, I decided to stop at the convenience store and pick up a few of my favorite treats. I was also experiencing physical pain, and since junk food was my drug of choice, I thought, "Go ahead and eat whatever you want today, surely something will help soothe your discomfort."

That was the epitome of another day of flawed thinking to justify my actions. It was also a day to worship the idol of my heart, which was food. Although I would never confess that I worshipped anyone or anything other than God, the fact that I used food as a constant source to soothe emotional discomfort or ease physical pain gave clarity to my relationship with food. Food distracted me from God and was the driving force behind my behavior. I spent time, energy, and resources pursuing and indulging in food. I chose to eat what I wanted. I chose to worship food. I chose to make it an idol.

The Almighty God created us to worship Him, so anything we put before the Lord is futile and will ultimately leave us dissatisfied and searching for more. Therefore, I urge you to seek the Lord with your whole heart and make God first at all costs. Worship the one who loves you most and knows you best. Let nothing else dominate your heart or your actions, and you will see that the Eternal God, who is above all and before all, will make your life complete.

*Little children, keep yourselves from idols
(false gods) - [from anything and everything
that would occupy the place in your heart due
to God, from any sort of substitute for Him that
would take first place in your life].
1 John 5:21 AMPC*

Prophetic Affirmations

I give the Lord first place in my life
I depend on God to satisfy my needs
I seek the Lord above all else

I give the Lord first place in my life
I depend on God to satisfy my needs
I seek the Lord above all else

*These affirmations are simple yet powerful.
Say them over and over until you do what you say.*

I give the Lord first place in my life
I depend on God to satisfy my needs
I seek the Lord above all else

Prayer for Today

Heavenly Father,
I come to You with a humble heart.
I come to You because You are God.

Forgive me for making food an idol.
Forgive me for not putting You first.

Heavenly Father,
I come to You because I know
You can help me with my struggles.
I come to You because You are my Lord.

May I always honor You.
May I always put You first,
in my heart and in my actions.
In Jesus' name, I pray

I am the Alpha and the Omega,
the Beginning and the End.
To the thirsty I will give water without cost.
Revelation 21:6 NIV

Whoever drinks the water I give them will
never thirst. Indeed, the water I give them
will become in them a spring of water
welling up to eternal life.
John 4:14 NIV

20

Is Anyone Thirsty?

Once upon a time, I was craving my favorite sandwich cookies, and I begin to make excuses to get some. I looked for them at the mini-mart, but none were on the shelf. I looked for them later when I went to get my mother something from the store, but I did not find them. I remember thinking, "Why are you looking for cookies that do not benefit your health? Why are you spending money on something that ultimately works against your good?" I do not know if I was craving sugar, mindlessly eating, or trying to fill some emotional void. Whatever the reason, I had surrendered to my whims and chased the superficial quick fix I so often succumbed to in the past.

In Isaiah 55:1-2 NLT, the prophet presents the question, "Is anyone thirsty? [If so] Come and drink even you who have no money. Why pay for food that does you no good?" I admit I was thirsty. I was thirsty for God, longing for fulfillment, and searching for purpose. Although I chased after cookies, I was fully aware that the momentary gratification that food brings (let alone a pack of sandwich cookies made with non-essential ingredients) could not begin to compare with the presence and power of the Almighty God.

Our heavenly Father knows what lies beneath the surface of our cravings, and He is more than able to complete what is lacking, fill every void, and heal the brokenness in our lives. Search for God. Let your soul delight in Him and let the Lord of the heavens and the earth fill you until you thirst no more.

As a deer longs for a stream of
cool water, so I long for you, O God.
I thirst for you the living God. When can
I go and worship in your presence?
Psalm 42:1-2 GNT

Prophetic Affirmations

I long for God
I thirst for the living God
I long for God's presence
I long for God to fill the void in me

Say the words over and over.
Be blessed by the words of your mouth.

I long for God
I thirst for the living God
I long for God's presence
I long for God to fill the void in me

I long for God
I thirst for the living God
I long for God's presence
I long for God to fill the void in me

Prayer for Today

Lord of lords and King of kings,
You are my God.
I search for You.
I thirst for You, like someone
in a dry, empty land
where there is no water.
Psalm 63:1 NCV

Fill me, Lord, with Your peace.
Heal the brokenness in me.
Fill me with Your glory and Your power.
Fill me with Your holy presence.
Fill me until I thirst no more.
In Jesus' name, I pray

Don't copy the behavior and customs of this world, but let God transform you into a new person by changing the way you think. Then you will learn to know God's will for you, which is good and pleasing and perfect.
Romans 12:2 NLT

21

It Matters

Sometimes we put off for tomorrow what we can do today because we think, "One more time won't matter. If I overeat one more day what difference will it make - one more cookie, one more bowl of ice cream, one more bag of chips, one more serving of food…the day is almost over anyway…one more time won't matter."

But it does matter. Every action matters because everything we do has a cause and effect. When we are attentive to what we put in our bodies, God is pleased and blesses our obedience. Consequently, if we are not careful, that one more bite, that one more unhealthy meal, or that one more act of disobedience, may be the one that denies us access to the greater things God has planned for us. We must also remember that the devil loves it when we procrastinate. He glories in the fact that we perpetually do the things that break down our bodies and hinder us from receiving heaven's best.

Every time we obey, it matters. Every time we say, "yes" to God's will and "no" to the things of the world, it matters. It may seem small or insignificant at the time, but when we choose to do what is best for our health and persevere against the demands and temptations of our flesh, it matters. Our obedience matters, and it is monumental to the plans and purposes of God.

Therefore, the next time you think, "One more time won't matter," remind yourself that everything matters to God, and if it matters to God, it should matter to you.

"Well done, my good servant!" his master replied.
"Because you have been trustworthy in a very
small matter, take charge of ten cities."
Luke 19:17 NIV

Prophetic Affirmations

It matters when I cut my portions in half
It matters when I exercise self-control
It matters when I eat only enough to sustain myself
It matters every time I do what is best for my body

It matters when I eat a balanced meal
It matters when I resist going back for seconds
It matters when I lay aside sugary desserts
It matters every time I do what is best for my body

It matters when I honor the Lord with what I eat
It matters every time I do what is best for my body

It matters every time you speak words of
encouragement. It matters every time you
speak words that give you strength.
Keep speaking. It matters!

Prayer for Today

Heavenly Father,
You are worthy of praise.
Blessed is the one who trusts in You.

Heavenly Father,
I want to eat healthier.
I want to make better choices.
I want to have control over my eating habits,
but sometimes my actions say differently.

Please give me a desire greater than words alone.
Please give me the grace to always say "yes" to
Jesus and the strength to say "no" to the world.
In Jesus' name, I pray

The command that I am giving you today is
not too difficult or beyond your reach.
It is not up in the sky. You do not have to ask,
'Who will go up and bring it down for us, so that
we can hear it and obey it?' Nor is it on the other
side of the ocean. You do not have to ask, 'Who will
go across the ocean and bring it to us, so that we
may hear it and obey it?' No, it is here with you.
You know it and can quote it, so just do it!
Deuteronomy 30:11-14 GNT, MSG

22

Just Do It

Even if you doubt a change will ever come
Even if you think the process is way too long
Even if you feel like the battle is too hard
God empowered you to overcome, so "Just do it!"

Even if you fear temptation may get the best of you
Even if you feel you may never do as you should
Even if you think the goal is too difficult to achieve
God equipped you to succeed, so "Just do it!"

Even if you fall short in sticking to a plan
Even if you think you may not make it to the end
Even if your best intentions still find you off the path
God created you to win, so "Just do it!"

Eat with restraint
Exercise self-control
"Just do it!"

Take care of your body
Eat as you should
Invest in your health
"Just do it!"

*Don't you realize that your body is the temple
of the Holy Spirit, who lives in you and was
given to you by God? You do not belong to
yourself, for God bought you with a high price.
So you must honor God with your body.
1 Corinthians 6:19-20 NLT*

Prophetic Affirmations

I will eat with restraint
I will exercise self-control
I will take care of my body
I will invest in my health

*Keep speaking. Inspire yourself by
what you say. Just do it!*

I will eat with restraint
I will exercise self-control
I will take care of my body
I will invest in my health

I will eat with restraint
I will exercise self-control
I will take care of my body
I will invest in my health

Prayer for Today

Lord of Heaven,
creator of all living things,
sustainer of everything that exists,
I owe You my life.

I trust You, Lord.
You are God Almighty.
I depend on You, Lord.
You are the Most High God.
You are the Everlasting Father.
You are my Lord and my God.
I worship You, and only You.
In Jesus' name

Tick-tock Tick-tock
Do you hear the clock?
Wake up and get up,
For tomorrow holds no guarantee.
Today is the day to decide how you will eat.
Wake up before the clock ticks your life away.
Wake up and do what you know to do today.

23

Let This Be the Day

How many times have you told yourself, "I will start my diet on Monday, after the holidays, the day after my birthday, or some other significant date," and commenced to eating all you could before that day came? How many times did that day come and go?

Many of us endeavoring to change the way we eat have probably experienced thoughts like these at one time or another. Regrettably, the "tomorrow mentality" can turn into weeks, months, years, and sometimes an entire lifetime. It also turns into extra pounds, unwanted illnesses, and life not lived to the fullest.

Putting off for another time what we can do right now will find us pulling all sorts of excuses out of our hats. Keep in mind that procrastination leads to a weak resolve and a place of stagnancy. We may drag our feet, but time waits for no one. The opportunity to eat better is now, for who knows, but God, what tomorrow will bring.

Celebrate your birthday and enjoy the holidays with family and friends. Have a treat on the weekend. You do not have to deny yourself small pleasures. Just the same, do not let some random date determine when you will love yourself enough to take care of your body.

Let this be the day that you stop procrastinating and do what is beneficial for your health. Let this be the day that you give your body what it needs, not what it wants. Let this be the day that you exercise self-control and say "no" to mindless eating, and let this be the day that you wake up and eat as you should.

If you wait for perfect conditions,
you will never get anything done.
Ecclesiastes 11:4 TLB

Prophetic Affirmations

Today I will take care of my body
Today I will exercise self-control
Today I will invest in my health

Meditate on the affirmations.
Repeat them until you believe what you say.

Today I will take care of my body
Today I will exercise self-control
Today I will invest in my health

Speak the words again.
Resolve to do what you hear.

Today I will take care of my body
Today I will exercise self-control
Today I will invest in my health

Prayer for Today

Sovereign Lord,
Holy and Righteous God,
I praise Your holy name.

Thank You for today.
Thank You for giving me
another chance to obey.

Forgive me, for I have put off doing the
right thing way too long, and I have laid
aside wisdom too many times to
satisfy unhealthy desires.

Please increase my faith to do well.
Please help me to honor my life.
In Jesus' name, I pray

Blessed the man, blessed the woman, who listens
to me, awake and ready for me each morning.
Proverbs 8:34 MSG

Mark a life of discipline and live wisely;
don't squander your precious life.
Proverbs 8:33 MSG

24

Mindless Mornings

Most mornings, I wake up focused and ready to go. However, there was a time when I woke up thinking about what I could or could not eat more than anything else. Had I written down my proposed diet plan, and if I had, was I supposed to start on that particular day? Had I made some agreement with God that I would give up sweets, and if I had, did I include the scones at the coffee shop? Had I promised myself that I would stop eating chips and popcorn and if so, did that include the tortilla chips usually served at a Mexican restaurant?

I am not exactly sure what I was doing during those times, but I do know that my idea of a diet plan lacked conviction and commitment. Looking back, my desire to eat right resembled wishful thinking rather than a well-thought-out plan. Instead of listening to wisdom and making sound decisions, I chose mindless, ineffectual thoughts to cloud my judgment and get me off the path of purpose.

The good news is that God never gave up on me nor allowed me to give up on myself. He encouraged me as I continued to stumble and admonished me as I failed to obey. He strengthened me in my struggles and empowered me to remain steadfast, even as I wobbled. Eventually, my desire for good health became stronger than my weakness for overeating. My focus on food did diminish, but not until I consistently meditated on the scriptures, spoke words of life over myself, and committed to a plan. It was only then that gaining control over my eating habits became more of a reality than just wishful thinking.

I am wisdom, and I have good judgment.
I also have knowledge and good sense.
Proverbs 8:12 NCV

The one who carefully seeks me in everyday things
and delays action until my way is apparent, that one
will find true happiness. For when he recognizes and
follows me, he finds a peaceful and satisfying life.
Proverbs 8:34-35 VOICE

Prophetic Affirmations

I wake up ready for wisdom
I seek wisdom in everyday things
I recognize wisdom, and I am satisfied
I follow wisdom, and I am at peace

Speak the words again.
Increase your faith by what you hear.

I wake up ready for wisdom
I seek wisdom in everyday things
I recognize wisdom, and I am satisfied
I follow wisdom, and I am at peace

Prayer for Today

You are worthy, oh God,
to receive glory and honor and power.
For you created all things, and they exist
because you created what you pleased.
Revelations 4:11 NLT

When I call Your name,
You reveal Yourself to me.
When I call Your name,
You are there, waiting to give me wisdom.

Apart from You, I can do nothing.
But with You working in me, for me,
and through me, I can do all things.
In Jesus' name

Therefore, dear brothers and sisters, you have
no obligation to do what your sinful nature
urges you to do. For if you live by its dictates,
you will die. But if through the power of the Spirit
you put to death the deeds of your sinful nature,
you will live. For all who are led by the
Spirit of God are children of God.
Romans 8:12-14 NLT

25

Never-Ending Temptations

Have you noticed that on the day you decide to start a diet, stop eating fast food, lower your carb intake, or refrain from eating sweets, is the very day that temptations seem more frequent than usual?

For instance, an old acquaintance calls you out of the blue and invites you to dinner, so you put off starting your diet to another day. Maybe a co-worker brings in gourmet pastries, throwing a wrench in your resolve to lay aside sugary foods. Or the boss decides to take the staff to a Mexican restaurant for an appreciation lunch, and who can diet when you start your meal with chips and salsa? My personal favorites are the days I said I would eat better and either a student knocks at the door selling candy, my sister shows up with pizza, or a friend surprises me with a Frappuccino from Starbucks. I forgot I had even planned to diet the morning I walked in the kitchen and my mother was frying chicken and potatoes for a family gathering.

Although these situations are tempting, we cannot blame anyone for our lack of commitment. James 1:14 CEV tells us that, "We are tempted by our own desires that drag us off and trap us."

With that in mind, determine to stick to a plan until you reach your goal. There will be distractions, and you will have off days. Resolve to stay alert, maintain your course, and hold fast to 1 Corinthians 10:13 TLB that says, "No temptation is irresistible. You can trust God to keep the temptation from becoming so strong that you can't stand up against it, for He has promised this and will do what He says."

*So prepare your minds for action and exercise
self-control... live as God's obedient children.
Don't slip back into your old ways of
living to satisfy your own desires.
1 Peter 1:13-14 NLT*

Prophetic Affirmations

I honor my body
I think before I eat
I prepare my mind for action
I exercise self-control

Repeat the words once more.

I honor my body
I think before I eat
I prepare my mind for action
I exercise self-control

Repeat them until you do what you say!

I honor my body
I think before I eat
I prepare my mind for action
I exercise self-control

Prayer for Today

Dear God,
master of all things.
You are my strength and my hope.
In You alone, I put my trust.

Please help me to stop and think before I eat.
Help me to resist temptation and to hold
fast to 1 Corinthians 10:13 TLB that says
"No temptation is irresistible."

Help me to walk in wisdom.
Help me to exercise self-control.
Help me to honor my body.
Help me to honor You.
In Jesus' name, I pray

Give your body what it
needs and say "no" to
Obesity
Low self-image
Diminishing health
A shortened life span.

Give your body what it needs
and LIVE.

26

Nicole's Story

I weigh 245 pounds. My self-esteem is low, and my self-image is even lower. I can hardly look in the mirror without feeling disgusted at myself. I have no energy, and I lack the motivation to do anything, except think about my next meal. I look like I am in my first trimester of pregnancy. I cannot cross my legs. Putting on pants has turned into a job. Mobility is difficult, clothes are too tight, and several body parts are hurting from inactivity and overeating. Already on medication for high blood pressure, heart disease, and glucose levels indicating I am prediabetic, I fear the damage I am doing to my health. My prayer is that God will help me. I know that I cannot make it on my own.

Nicole is not alone in her struggle, for many have become slaves to food. None of us intentionally want to eat uncontrollably or sacrifice our health for a plate of food. Nevertheless, if we keep doing things the same way, we will indeed yield the same results. Patience, hard work, and consistency are vital to our success and our recovery. Bear in mind that our eating habits will not change overnight, but they will not change at all unless we do something different.

Take everything to the Lord. Be honest as you present your fears, needs, and desires to Him. Trust God to heal you emotionally and physically, and to give you the strength to eat in moderation. It does not matter how overweight you are or how long you have allowed food to dominate your days. You can still live your best life now and achieve a healthier lifestyle with God on your side.

Be strong in the Lord [be empowered through
your union with Him]; draw your strength from Him
[that strength which His boundless might provides].
Ephesians 6:10 AMPC

Prophetic Affirmations

I am strong in the Lord
I draw my strength from the Lord
I am empowered through my union with God

There is power in the Word of God. Keep speaking.

I am strong in the Lord
I draw my strength from the Lord
I am empowered through my union with God

There is power in what you say. Keep speaking.

I am strong in the Lord
I draw my strength from the Lord
I am empowered through my union with God

Prayer for Today

Lord of lords and King of kings,
Supreme Ruler of the heavens and the earth,
I repent for my lack of restraint and self-indulgence.
Please forgive me for abusing my body.
Please forgive me for dishonoring my life.

Deliver me from this struggle, Lord.
Give me the courage to live my best life now.
I am weak, but You are my strength.
Increase my faith, Lord.
Help me to trust You more.
In Jesus' name, I pray

And I am convinced that nothing can ever separate us from God's love. Neither death nor life, neither angels nor demons, neither our fears for today nor our worries about tomorrow—not even the powers of hell can separate us from God's love. No power in the sky above or in the earth below—indeed, nothing in all creation will ever be able to separate us from the love of God that is revealed in Christ Jesus our Lord.
Romans 8:38-39 NLT

27

No Greater Love

God is love, which means He can only demonstrate love. His love is incomparable, immeasurable, and eternal. It is a mighty love with no beginning and no end. God loves beyond conditions and circumstances, power and personalities, and there is no partiality with Him. He loves each one of us uniquely, completely, and perfectly.

God's love is so great that He sent Jesus to die for us. If we could only comprehend the magnitude of His love and mercy for us, maybe then we could see ourselves as the magnificent creatures He created us to be and honor the love of God by honoring our bodies.

To honor our bodies means to take care of them to the best of our ability. This includes (1) eating foods that contain vital nutrients versus filling ourselves with empty calories, (2) getting up from the table when we feel satisfied instead of stuffing ourselves just because we can, and (3) standing firm when unhealthy cravings persist, instead of mindlessly eating everything that appeals to our taste buds.

Because God loves us and is concerned with every element of our lives, He is faithful to help us achieve good eating habits. The God of all might and power will help us because He loves us. He will show us what to do because He loves us. Our heavenly Father will strengthen us in our weaknesses and help us to resist temptation because He loves us. God will teach us how to love ourselves because He loves us. There is no greater love than the all-encompassing, all-empowering love of God, and He wants the best for us.

No one hates his own body but lovingly cares for it.
Ephesians 5:29 TLB

Prophetic Affirmations

I love myself more than mindless eating
I love myself more than a delicious dessert
I love myself more than late night snacking
I love myself more than anything I could eat

Say these words over and over until you
love yourself enough to treat your body well.

I love myself more than mindless eating
I love myself more than a delicious dessert
I love myself more than late night snacking
I love myself more than anything I could eat

I love myself more than mindless eating
I love myself more than a delicious dessert
I love myself more than late night snacking
I love myself more than anything I could eat

Prayer for Today

Heavenly Father,
You are the only living God and
I am blessed to call You my Lord.

Thank You for loving me and for
teaching me to love myself.

Please help me to honor You, Lord.
Help me to honor the love You have for me.
Help me to honor my body.
Help me to honor my life.
In Jesus' name, I pray

Do not give the devil a way to defeat you.
Ephesians 4:27 NCV

Use every piece of God's armor to resist the
enemy whenever he attacks, and when it is
all over, you will still be standing up.
Ephesians 6:13 TLB

28

No Temptation Too Great

According to Matthew 4:1-10 NIV, "Jesus was led by the Spirit into the wilderness to be tempted by the devil. After fasting forty days and forty nights, he was hungry. The tempter came to him and said, 'If you are the Son of God, tell these stones to become bread.' Jesus answered, 'It is written: 'Man shall not live on bread alone, but on every word that comes from the mouth of God.'"

Again, the devil took him to a very high mountain and showed him all the kingdoms of the world and their splendor. "All this I will give you," he said, "if you will bow down and worship me." Jesus said to him, "Away from me, Satan! For it is written: 'Worship the Lord your God, and serve him only.'"

The devil is cunning, and he is unrelenting. He will try to sabotage your weight loss goals, destroy your endeavor to eat healthier, and distract you in any way he can. He will attack your mind with thoughts of defeat and prey on your weaknesses. "Stay alert! Watch out for our great enemy, the devil. He prowls around like a roaring lion, looking for someone to devour" (1 Peter 5:8 NLT).

Equip yourself to overcome the devil's lies by meditating on the scriptures. The words you rehearse will rise in your spirit when you need them most. The Word works. Have faith in its power. It is alive. It is true and it is your weapon against the adversary. Do what Jesus did. Speak the Word, resist the devil, and experience victory over every temptation set up against you.

*The temptations in your life are no different
from what others experience. And God is faithful.
He will not allow the temptation to be more than you
can stand. When you are tempted, he will show
you a way out so that you can endure.*
1 Corinthians 10:13 NLT

Prophetic Affirmations

I can endure temptation
I can prevail over the tricks of the enemy
God is faithful to show me a way out
No temptation is too great

I can endure temptation
I can prevail over the tricks of the enemy
God is faithful to show me a way out
No temptation is too great

Increase your faith by the words you speak.
Change your life by what you say.

I can endure temptation
I can prevail over the tricks of the enemy
God is faithful to show me a way out
No temptation is too great

Prayer for Today

Heavenly Father,
You are the Lord God Almighty
from whom all blessings flow.

Forgive me for not speaking
Your Word when tempted.
Forgive me for not walking
in the authority I have in Christ.

Please increase my faith to walk in victory,
and empower me to prevail over the enemy.
Be merciful to me, God, and help me to obey.

Your grace is all I need.
In Jesus' name

I am the Vine; you are the branches.
The one who remains in Me and I in him
bears much fruit, for [otherwise] apart
from Me[that is, cut off from vital union
with Me] you can do nothing.
John 15:5 AMP

And we know that all that happens to
us is working for our good if we love God
and are fitting into his plans.
Romans 8:28 TLB

29

Not Without God

Newsflash!! If you do not spend time with God…if you do not study the scriptures…if you do not take time to pray…if you do not trust the Holy Spirit to help you, you will neither have the strength nor the resolve to gain dominion over your eating habits. "For apart from God, we can do nothing" (John 15:5 NLT).

We need God to win. We need Him to fight our battles. We need Him to strengthen us from within and give us enduring power to do what we know we should. We need God, who works all things out for our good, to walk alongside us and show us how to live the abundant life He planned for us to live.

God never intended for us to exist without Him nor overcome bad habits by ourselves. For this reason, we must nurture our relationship with the Lord. Spend time marveling at creation, and you will see God. Sit quietly and think about His goodness, and you will encounter God. Read the Bible so you will know His thoughts. Talk to God and rest assured He will reveal Himself to you.

When you make a healthy choice, thank God for helping you to do so. When you fall short, ask for forgiveness, and for strength to do better the next time. Whatever you do, include God. "Draw near to Him, and He will draw near to you" (James 4:8 NKJV). He will empower you to change, equip you to win, and help you to honor Him with what you eat and what you drink. Without God, you can do nothing, but with God, you can accomplish great things.

Draw near to God and He will draw near to you.
James 4:8 NKJV

Prophetic Affirmations

I draw near to God
God draws near to me
God helps me to win my battles
God helps me to overcome all things

Say the words again.
Recognize that you are speaking absolute truth.

I draw near to God
God draws near to me
God helps me to win my battles
God helps me to overcome all things

Say the words again and let the truth change you.

I draw near to God
God draws near to me
God helps me to win my battles
God helps me to overcome all things

Prayer for Today

Most High God,
I have fallen short so many times
in my efforts to change my eating habits.
Forgive me for trying to do it my way.

Please help me to trust You more
and to do things Your way.

Thank You for Your faithfulness.
Thank You for Your grace.
Thank You for Your strength.
Thank You for everything You do.
In Jesus' name, I pray

*Dear friends, do you think you'll get
anywhere in this if you learn all the
right words but never do anything?*
James 2:14 MSG

*Well-spoken words bring satisfaction;
well-done work has its own reward.*
Proverbs 12:14 MSG

30

One Step at a Time

Sometimes we lack the courage to eat as we should. Sometimes the food choices before us are not as healthy as we would like. There are also times when we are just lazy and unwillingly to do what it takes to change the way we eat.

We can spend endless hours talking and thinking about doing the right thing. We can pray, make a great plan, and mentally position ourselves for success. But until we actively participate in creating and maintaining a healthier environment, nothing much will change. Yes, our desires may become stronger, our plans more strategic, and our prayers more intense. But if we do not monitor our portions and make wiser food choices, the change we desire will never become a reality. We cannot think ourselves into a desired outcome, but watching our carbs, cutting out the sugar, and lowering our sodium intake will positively impact our health. We must physically do something different if we want to achieve a change.

Proverbs 13:4 AMP says, "The soul (appetite) of the lazy person craves and gets nothing [for lethargy overcomes ambition]." Therefore, desire an appetite for success and take a small step toward a healthier lifestyle. Keep in mind that the longer you lay around thinking about what you should or could be doing, the easier it becomes to do nothing.

Make a plan and commit to it. Choose a single goal within your plan and work towards it. Take one step at a time and get closer to your goal. Take one step at a time and change your life for good.

How long will you lie down, O lazy one?
When will you arise from your sleep
[and learn self-discipline]?
Proverbs 6:9 AMP

Prophetic Affirmations

I will learn self-discipline
I will do what is right for my body
I will rise up and take a step for my health

Keep speaking until you believe what you say.

I will learn self-discipline
I will do what is right for my body
I will rise up and take a step for my health

Keep speaking until you do what you hear.

I will learn self-discipline
I will do what is right for my body
I will rise up and take a step for my health

Prayer for Today

Maker of heaven and earth,
God of all power and might,
there is nothing impossible for You.

Please help me to exercise self-control,
to do what is right for my body,
and to invest in my health,
one step at a time.

Please help me to set goals that line
up with Your purpose and give me
the strength to stay on task.

Thank You for never giving up on me.
Thank You for Your lovingkindness.
In Jesus' name, I pray

Make every effort to add to your faith
goodness; and to goodness, knowledge;
and to knowledge, self-control;
and to self-control, perseverance;
and to perseverance, godliness.
2 Peter 1:5-6 NIV

31

Persevere in the Process

It would be great if everything would go quick and easy once we made up our minds to eat healthier and get our bodies in order. The pounds would fly off, inches would disappear like magic, cravings would go away, and overcoming temptation would be no problem at all. Yes, it would be great, but it is not realistic. We did not develop bad eating habits overnight nor allow food to become our drug of choice in a few days. Likewise, to change the way we eat is a process that requires self-control and perseverance.

Step by step, with one foot in front of the other, we can develop healthy habits. The important thing is that when we stumble, we do not become so discouraged that we doubt the process and stop altogether. We cannot get to the next level in any aspect of life if we allow our mistakes to paralyze us. Instead, we must learn from our experiences, commit to the journey, and trust God even more. The Lord is with us, and He will cause us to triumph.

Persevere in your efforts to honor God by doing what is best for your body. God is waiting to bless you in ways that can only happen when you walk in faith and stay on the pathway of obedience. Persevere until you can resist the tricks of the enemy and be watchful because your adversary waits for opportunities to impede your success. Persevere until you can rise above nagging cravings and desires. God will give you what you need to endure every temptation. Persevere because it is a process. Persevere because it glorifies God.

You need to persevere so that when you have done
the will of God, you will receive what He has promised.
Hebrews 10:36 NIV

Prophetic Affirmations

I will persevere until I do what is best for my body
I will persevere until I maintain a healthy lifestyle
I will persevere because it is the will of God

I will persevere until I do what is best for my body
I will persevere until I maintain a healthy lifestyle
I will persevere because it is the will of God

Close your eyes and meditate on the words
"I will persevere." Let the words permeate
your thoughts. Speak them over and over
and be empowered by what you hear.

I will persevere until I do what is best for my body
I will persevere until I maintain a healthy lifestyle
I will persevere because it is the will of God

Prayer for Today

Dear God,
I know I can do all things with You on my side,
although sometimes the process seems so long.
Sometimes it seems as if I am not going to
be able to overcome this struggle at all.

But since these are only feelings
and lack of confidence in myself,
I surrender my inadequacies to You.

In faith, I know You are helping me,
so in faith, I will persevere.

Thank You for Your love and Your grace.
In Jesus' name, I pray

Ask the Lord to bless your plans,
and you will be successful
in carrying them out.
Proverbs 16:3 GNT

It is pleasant to see plans develop.
Proverbs 13:19 TLB

32

Plan to Prosper

When we plan, we work with a vision;
Which is the essence of sound decisions.

When we plan, it helps us to see,
That staying on course will get us to our destiny.

When we plan, it provides direction,
Which gives us clarity and a purposeful perspective.

When we plan, and there is movement,
Hope becomes a reality as we see improvement.

And when we plan there is an expectation;
To believe in a good outcome fortifies our determination.

A successful plan is agreeing with God's plan and choosing to walk
in the path that He has predestined for our lives. His plan includes
exercising self-control, disciplining our bodies, and honoring Him
with what we eat and what we drink. Because this is God's plan for
us, we never have to worry that we are alone in the process. He is with
us every step of the way, strengthening, equipping, and leading us to
victory. As we follow and obey, we will prosper, not only in our eating
habits but in all things, which is the will of God!

Beloved, I pray that you may prosper in all things
and be in health, just as your soul prospers.
3 John 2 NKJV

Prophetic Affirmations

I plan to prosper in all things
I plan to be in good health
I plan to take care of my body
I plan to eat as I should

I plan to prosper in all things
I plan to be in good health
I plan to take care of my body
I plan to eat as I should

Keep talking about your plan.
Say what you want to do until you do it.

I plan to prosper in all things
I plan to be in good health
I plan to take care of my body
I plan to eat as I should

Prayer for Today

Holy and Awesome God,
You alone know the plans and purposes for
my life and I know they do not include overeating,
overindulging, or dishonoring my body in any way.

Holy and Awesome God,
I put my trust in You.
You know the way that I should go.
You alone can lead me to victory,
and cause me to prosper in every area.

Help me to follow You, Lord.
Help me to do what You say.
Help me to live the life You planned for me.
In Jesus' name, I pray

Jesus answered, "'Love the Lord your God with all your heart, with all your soul, and with all your mind.' This is the greatest and the most important commandment."
Matthew 22:37-38 GNT

For everything comes from God alone. Everything lives by his power, and everything is for his glory. To him be glory evermore.
Romans 11:36 TLB

33

Put God First

God can do anything. Nothing is impossible for Him, and He is ready at all times and in every way to help us rise above our struggles. But we have to give the Sovereign Lord, creator of the universe, His rightful place in our hearts and put Him first in everything we do.

Put God first by acknowledging Him before you eat. Give thanks for His provision and pray along the lines from Proverbs 30:8 NLT that says, "Lord, give me just enough to satisfy my needs." Yes, the Holy Spirit will reveal to you when you have eaten enough to meet your physical needs. It is up to you to listen and obey.

Put God first by honoring your life and treating your body with love. Give up those things that are damaging to your health. Do not forfeit your well-being for some tasty morsel that only gratifies as long as the flavor lasts, but learn what foods are good for your body and eat those things instead.

Put God first by allowing Him to ease the anxieties of your heart. Pray about everything and avoid using food as a means to cope with unpleasant emotions. Lean on God. He knows what you need, and He is more than able to comfort you at all times and in every way.

Put God first. He will guide you with His eye upon you. He will empower you to succeed and provide a way out of every temptation. God will fight your battles, and He will never abandon you.

Put God first. Honor Him and seek His will, above all else. Give God first place in your heart and prosper in everything you do.

*In everything you do, put God first, and he will
direct you and crown your efforts with success.*
Proverbs 3:6 TLB

Prophetic Affirmations

I put God first by acknowledging Him before I eat
I put God first by treating my body well
I put God first by seeking His will above all else

Repeat the affirmations and pause after each sentence.

I put God first by acknowledging Him before I eat
I put God first by treating my body well
I put God first by seeking His will above all else

Repeat the affirmations several times a day.
Repeat them until you do what you say.

I put God first by acknowledging Him before I eat
I put God first by treating my body well
I put God first by seeking His will above all else

Prayer for Today

King of kings and Lord of lords,
You are the reason I exist.

Because of You, I have breath of life.
Because of You, there is purpose to my days.

Thank You for empowering me to succeed.
Thank You for fighting my battles.
Thank You for never abandoning me.

You are the Lord God Almighty
and there is none like You.
In Jesus' name

I, Wisdom, will make the hours of your day
more profitable and the years of your life
more fruitful. Wisdom is its own reward.
Proverbs 9:11-12 TLB

Careful planning puts you ahead
in the long run; hurry and scurry
puts you further behind.
Proverbs 21:5 MSG

34

Ready or Not

It is easy to get off track if you do not plan. For example, there may be times you allow yourself to get famished, and you have nothing prepared to eat. You grab whatever is quick while thinking your way to a healthier choice. Sometimes you end up settling for chips or sugary snacks because you are too hungry and weak to make a good decision.

Cooking meals ahead of time and stocking your kitchen with healthy foods will keep you motivated and inspire you to stay on course. You also have to build yourself up spiritually, mentally, and emotionally by praying and listening to God, speaking affirmations, and meditating on the scriptures. Keep in mind that the scriptures you study are the ones that will rise in your spirit when you need them most. Likewise, the prophetic affirmations you rehearse are the ones that will flow easily from your lips during times of temptation or when you are battling self-sabotaging thoughts.

Plan to succeed, because ready or not, temptations are going to come. Prepare your meals beforehand and pray often. Eliminate the junk from your kitchen and replace them with healthy snacks. Set boundaries for yourself and refuse to yield to random decisions. Visualize the results you want to see and remain focused on your goal.

I know that planning is not foolproof. You will have unexpected invites, resort to mindless eating, or have an off day, but the more diligent you are in working a plan, the more routine it will become, and the closer you will get to achieving a healthier lifestyle.

Commit your actions to the Lord,
and your plans will succeed.
Proverbs 16:3 NLT

You're blessed when you stay on course, walking steadily
on the road revealed by God. You're blessed when you
follow his directions, doing your best to find him.
Psalm 119:1-2 MSG

Prophetic Affirmations

I am blessed because I do my best to find God
I am blessed because I follow God's directions
I am blessed because I stay on course
I am blessed because my plans will succeed

Keep speaking about your blessings.
Change your life by what you say!

I am blessed because I do my best to find God
I am blessed because I follow God's directions
I am blessed because I stay on course
I am blessed because my plans will succeed

Prayer for Today

Holy God,
You are the master planner,
perfect in all Your ways.

Thank You for helping me to plan, and to do
what it takes to achieve a healthy lifestyle.

Thank You for Your promise to help me succeed.
Thank You for being the voice behind me
saying "This is the way, walk in it."

I owe my life to You, God.
Thank You for everything!
In Jesus' name, I pray

*Let us strip off anything that slows us down
or holds us back, and especially those sins
that wrap themselves so tightly around our feet
and trip us up; and let us run with patience
the particular race that God has set before us.*
Hebrews 12:1 TLB

35

Run Your Race

If you wanted to complete a marathon, do you think you could show up on the day of the race and run it successfully without proper training or conditioning? Do you think your body could withstand the long distance without any prior short distance runs leading up to the race? Do you think you could run comfortably without drinking enough water? Or stuff yourself the night before with junk food and have the energy you need to complete the race? Do you honestly think that your body could sustain 26.2 miles of running if you merely read literature or watched videos on marathons?

While it is not impossible to complete a marathon without preparation or training, it is impractical. You would likely get dehydrated and suffer from cramps or some other physical injury. It is also probable that you would lack the mental fortitude to keep running when every part of your body was screaming to stop.

Likewise, we cannot complete our race to change our eating habits without preparation or training. Prayer is essential, and meditating on the Word is a must. Therefore, find scriptures on self-control, temptation, and perseverance. Gain knowledge about nutrition and the different effects food has on the body. Commit to an eating plan, exercise, and take vitamins, if necessary. Prepare your mind, body, and spirit so that you can run your race successfully. Remember that changing your eating habits is neither a sprint nor a marathon, but a lifetime journey with multiple rewards.

She equips herself with strength
[spiritual, mental and physical fitness for her
God-given task] and makes her arms strong.
Proverbs 31:17 AMP

Prophetic Affirmations

I am training my body to be at its best
I am working hard to keep my mind healthy
I am doing what it takes to stay spiritually strong
I am preparing myself for my God-given task

Keep speaking the scriptures for they are absolute truth.

I am training my body to be at its best
I am working hard to keep my mind healthy
I am doing what it takes to stay spiritually strong
I am preparing myself for my God-given task

Keep speaking and let the words inspire you.

I am training my body to be at its best
I am working hard to keep my mind healthy
I am doing what it takes to stay spiritually strong
I am preparing myself for my God-given task

Prayer for Today

Holy God,
You are the same yesterday, today and forever.
You are an ever-present help.
You are my rock and the one I trust.

Please help me to do everything I can
to stay physically, spiritually, and
mentally fit for my life's journey.
Please help me to run my race with faith
and to trust You every step of the way.

Thank You for helping me to achieve victory.
Thank You for helping me to
honor You with all that I do.
In Jesus' name, I pray

If you love life and want to live a good,
long time, then be careful what you say.
1 Peter 3:10 VOICE

Let the words of my mouth and
The meditation of my heart be
acceptable in Your sight, O Lord,
my strength and my Redeemer.
Psalm 19:14 NKJV

36

Say What You Pray

Proverbs 4:25 NCV tells us to "keep our eyes focused on what is right and look straight ahead to what is good." Although we may know what is right and good, sometimes we lose our way and find ourselves off course. That is why it is so important to begin our day by talking with our heavenly Father, telling Him our concerns, admitting our struggles, and sharing the secrets of our hearts.

It is just as important that the words we say in prayer align with the words we say to ourselves and others. For it is futile to spend time confessing to God the good we want to do and then turn around and speak contrary to what we pray. Why ask God for strength to overcome bad habits if you continue to tell yourself it is too hard to do? Or why share your desire to create a positive change in your life but consistently speak words of doubt and defeat?

Fill your mind with scriptures that validate who you are in Christ. Meditate on the promises and plans of God. Gain wisdom and insight into His character and learn what He expects of you. Find your purpose and destiny in the Word of God. Speak about those things and be inspired to live the life He ordained for you.

Search the scriptures and let them be your guide for prayer. Then turn your prayers into affirmations. In doing so, the words you speak will be consistent with the Word of God. God will honor what you say when you say what He says. Pray in faith, speak with confidence, and be blessed by the words of your mouth.

So Jesus answered and said to them, "Have faith in God. For assuredly, I say to you, whoever says to this mountain, 'Be removed and be cast into the sea,' and does not doubt in his heart, but believes that those things he says will be done, he will have whatever he says. Therefore, I say to you, whatever things you ask when you pray, believe that you receive them, and you will have them."
Mark 11:22-24 NKJV

Prophetic Affirmations

I have faith in God
I believe in the power of prayer
I believe in the power of words
I believe I can have what I say

I have faith in God
I believe in the power of prayer
I believe in the power of words
I believe I can have what I say

God will honor your words when they align with His will. Keep speaking until you have what you say.

Prayer for Today

Holy God,
You are the self-existing, self-sufficient,
ever-present, all-powerful, only living God,
and You show Yourself strong and mighty
in behalf of Your children.

Forgive me for the times
I have thought or spoken words of defeat.
Forgive me for the times
I have spoken words of unbelief.

May I always speak words of faith,
hope, purpose, and power.
In Jesus' name, I pray

An appetite for good brings much satisfaction.
Proverbs 13:25 MSG

How sweet are your words to my taste,
sweeter than honey to my mouth!
Psalm 119:103 NIV

37

Speak the Word

I remember a time I started an excellent regime of eliminating foods that did not edify my body, including but not limited to refined sugar, dairy, and gluten. My goal was to give my body what it needed, not what it wanted. I was so successful in this endeavor that I thought, "This is great, I have arrived. Praise God. My struggle is over."

Two months later, I found myself once again at square one of my quest to eat healthier. I realized even though I had seemingly discovered a program that worked well for me, I had failed to include the discipline of speaking the Word over this area of my life. Although one can succeed in any endeavor for a short period, the Lord showed me that without the power of His Word infusing my soul, I could only go so far in my own strength.

I encourage you to find an eating plan that works for you. More importantly, discover what the scriptures say and speak them over your life. Affirm yourself with statements that move you to action and keep you focused as you work towards your goal. Even if you repeat one or two lines, do it daily, when you wake up, before you go to bed, before you eat, for five minutes at a time or periodically throughout the day. Whatever you do, be consistent.

Create an atmosphere for change by the words of your mouth. Your eating habits will not turn around overnight. But if you consistently use your voice and speak life-giving words over yourself, it will change your thoughts and ultimately your actions.

Your words are what sustain me; they are
food to my hungry soul. They bring joy to my
sorrowing heart and delight me. How
proud I am to bear your name, O Lord.
Jeremiah 15:16 TLB

Prophetic Affirmations

God's words bring joy to my heart
God's words are food to my hungry soul
God's words give me hope and encouragement
God's words are what sustain me

Keep speaking. There is power in the scriptures,
and there is power in what you say!

God's words bring joy to my heart
God's words are food to my hungry soul
God's words give me hope and encouragement
God's words are what sustain me

God's words bring joy to my heart
God's words are food to my hungry soul
God's words give me hope and encouragement
God's words are what sustain me

Prayer for Today

Holy God,
You spoke and created the heavens and the earth.
You spoke and told the oceans how deep to go.
You spoke, and the mountains knew how tall to stand.
You spoke, and the sun and the moon came to be.

Holy God,
May the words I speak, create a change in me.
May the words I speak, transform my life for good.
May the words I speak, empower me to persevere.
May the words I speak, be pleasing to You.
In Jesus' holy name, I pray

Speak the Word
Until you make right food choices
Until you can turn down the desserts
Until you can walk away from the junk food

Speak the Word
Until you no longer eat late at night
Until you cease from feeding emotional voids
Until you stop eating just because you can

Speak the Word
Until you honor God's temple
Until you worship the Lord with your body
Until you know you have done your best

Speak the Word
Until you eat like you should!

38

Spiritual Menu

Breakfast
"I taste and see that God is good." (Psalm 34:8 NIV)

Morning Snack
"God fills my mouth with good things." (Psalm 103:5 TLB)

Lunch
"I draw my nourishment from the Lord." (Colossians 2:7 TLB)

Afternoon Snack
"I feed on His faithfulness." (Psalm 37:3 NKJV)

Dinner
"I have treasured the words of His mouth
more than my necessary food."
(Job 23:12 NKJV)

A daily regime of reading and meditating on the scriptures is powerful and effective. The scriptures teach us how to live and give us hope for our future. They strengthen us to do what we were born to do and equip us for godly living. Therefore, for breakfast, feed on the Word. With lunch, affirm yourself with truth. As part of your snack time, empower yourself with the Word. For dinner, say what God says.

I have treasured the words of His mouth
more than my necessary food.
Job 23:12 NKJV

Taste and see that the Lord is good;
Blessed is the man who trusts in Him!
Psalm 34:8 NKJV

Prophetic Affirmations

I treasure God's Word more than my daily food
I taste and see that the Lord is good
I trust in God, and I am blessed

Declare the scriptures over yourself morning,
noon, and night. It will change the way you think.
It will change the way you eat.

I treasure God's Word more than my daily food
I taste and see that the Lord is good
I trust in God, and I am blessed

I treasure God's Word more than my daily food
I taste and see that the Lord is good
I trust in God, and I am blessed

Prayer for Today

Dear God,
Your Word is true and eternal.
Your faithfulness is beyond measure.

Please give me a hunger for Jesus and
a fresh revelation of Your Word.
Satisfy me with Your truth.
Fill me with Your goodness.

Bless me, Lord, as I speak Your Word over my life.
Bless me as I empower myself to change.
In Jesus' name, I pray

May he give you the desire
of your heart and make all
your plans succeed.
Psalm 20:4 NIV

The Lord makes firm the steps of the
one who delights in him; though he
may stumble, he will not fall, for the
Lord upholds him with his hand.
Psalm 37:23-24 NIV

39

Stand for Something

There was a time in my life (for three days) that I went on several different diet plans per day. Yes, you read correctly. I started my morning with the Master Cleanse Lemonade Diet, which is a liquid-only diet/detoxification program consisting of a lemonade-like drink with cayenne pepper, salt-water, and an herbal laxative tea, which you were to drink for ten days. Two hours later, I switched to the Atkins Diet (low carbs, high protein). A few minutes later, I decided a couple of breakfast muffins would be okay, so I ate them while on the other two diet plans. Then I went to the store and successfully quoted scripture to overcome the temptation to buy sweets. A little later, I went out again, purchased some junk food, and happily devoured it. Throughout the day, I ate plenty of meat for protein and consumed lots of popcorn for my fiber intake. What a time of confusion! What a disaster for my body! Thank God it only lasted three days.

I know it seems unbelievable that I would submit my body to such turmoil. This experience, nonetheless, showed me that whether it is a three-day ball of confusion or a lifetime of bad choices, if you do not stand for something, you will fall for anything, and if you do not live with purpose and vision, you will go in any direction the wind blows.

Commit to a plan and stick to it until the plan works for you. Keep in mind that habits, whether good or bad, take time to develop. Therefore, pray often, ask God for wisdom, be firm with yourself, and stand up for your health.

If any of you needs wisdom, you should ask God for it.
He is generous to everyone and will give you wisdom
without criticizing you. But when you ask God, you must
believe and not doubt. Anyone who doubts is like a wave in
the sea, blown up and down by the wind. Such doubters are
thinking two different things at the same time, and they
cannot decide about anything they do. They should not
think they will receive anything from the Lord.
James 1:5-8 NCV

Prophetic Affirmations

I pray about my eating plan
I ask God for wisdom
I make a decision and I stick to it
I stand up for my health

Keep speaking until you do what you say.
Keep speaking until you change the way you eat!

I pray about my eating plan
I ask God for wisdom
I make a decision and I stick to it
I stand up for my health

Prayer for Today

Heavenly Father,
You are my Savior.
Forgive me, for I have stumbled so many times
because of indecisiveness and find myself
at the starting gate time and time again.

Heavenly Father,
You are my God.
Please help me to commit
to a plan and to finish what I start.
Please help me to live wisely
and to stand up for my health.

Heavenly Father,
You are my Lord.
May I honor You in all that I do.
In Jesus' name, I pray

It is not good for a person to be without knowledge, and he who hurries with his feet [acting impulsively and proceeding without caution or analyzing the consequences] sins (misses the mark).
Proverbs 19:2 AMP

40

Stop, Look & Listen

Before you take your next bite of food, stop and ask yourself, "Am I hungry or eating out of boredom? Do I need food for energy, or am I tired and need to rest? Am I eating to suppress some emotion, or am I eating just because I can?"

Stop long enough and pose these questions to yourself. "Am I doing what is best for my health? Am I exercising self-control or eating mindlessly without restraint? Am I honoring God with what I eat, or am I allowing food to dominate my life?"

Stop long enough and look at what you are eating. What is the calorie count? What is the breakdown of carbohydrates, fats, and proteins? Is it high in sodium or sugar? Is it organic, or loaded with additives, fillers, and artificial ingredients?

Look at what is on your plate? Is it portion controlled or some random amount of food? Do you see a balance of veggies and protein? Is it a home-cooked meal or take-out from a fast-food restaurant?

Stop long enough and listen to what your body is saying. Are you gaining weight, experiencing unhealthy cravings, having mood swings, lacking energy, or facing physical ailments? Listen to your body. It will tell you when enough is enough.

Stop long enough to pray and hear from God. Stop long enough to speak words of encouragement and strength. Stop long enough to think about what you are eating. Stop long enough until you decide to do what is best for your body.

Wise people think before they act.
Proverbs 13:16 NLT

Prophetic Affirmations

I will stop and think before I eat
I will stop and listen to what my body is saying
I will stop and do what is best for my health

Keep speaking these words of wisdom.

I will stop and think before I eat
I will stop and listen to what my body is saying
I will stop and do what is best for my health

Speak the words again.
Reshape your thoughts by what you say!

I will stop and think before I eat
I will stop and listen to what my body is saying
I will stop and do what is best for my health

Prayer for Today

Sovereign God,
You alone are holy.

Lord, sometimes I plow right into my day
without any thought about what I am going to eat,
so I end up eating whatever is handy, free, or desirable.

Please help me, Father, to stop and think,
to consider my health, and to make wise choices.
Please help me to honor You with what I eat.
Please help me to take care of my body.

To You, be all the glory, today and forever.
In Jesus' name, I pray

Not by might, nor by power,
but by my Spirit, says the Lord Almighty—
you will succeed because of my Spirit.
Zechariah 4:6 TLB

Weapons made to attack
you won't be successful;
words spoken against you
won't hurt at all.
Isaiah 54:17 CEV

41

Stop Self-Sabotage

Self-Sabotage walks alongside you, peering into the secrets of your heart. She watches for you to take your eyes off your purpose and surrender to the misconception that you do not deserve what you are trying to accomplish. She thrives off your fears and inadequacies and waits for a glimpse of vulnerability. At the opportune time, she cleverly whispers her words of destruction: "You will not make it, so go ahead and mess up. It is too late, so quit trying, or it is too hard, so why keep going? You will probably fail anyway."

Self-Sabotage seeks to minimize your motivation, undermine your efforts, and limit your progress. She is committed to exposing your weaknesses and uses the failures of your past to throw you off course and diminish your hopes for a successful future.

Self-Sabotage is a crafty and daunting opponent, but she is not invincible. You can overcome her with spiritual truths and a resolve to accomplish what you set out to do. Recognize her tactics and depend upon the Lord's power to keep you in a winning position. Trust that God, who transcends all things, will show you common stumbling blocks and equip you with strategies for success.

Stop Self-Sabotage with the Word of God. Saturate yourself with scriptures on strength, power, and victory until you see yourself from God's perspective. Speak truth over yourself morning, noon and night. Remember, you were born to succeed, and you can do all things through Christ who gives you strength.

Finally, believers, whatever is true, whatever is honorable and worthy of respect, whatever is right and confirmed by God's word, whatever is pure and wholesome, whatever is lovely and brings peace, whatever is admirable and of good repute; if there is any excellence, if there is anything worthy of praise, think continually on these things [center your mind on them, and implant them in your heart].
Philippians 4:8 AMP

Prophetic Affirmations

I let go of negative self-talk
I release self-doubt and self-sabotage
I meditate on things that are true
I think about things that bring me peace
I center my mind on things that are pure
I think about things that are worthy of respect
I think about things that are admirable
I think about things that are good

Align your thoughts with the Word of God.
Say what the scriptures say.
Keep speaking until you do what you hear.

Prayer for Today

Heavenly Father,
maker of all things visible and invisible,
You are a great God with wonderful plans for me.
Help me to remember that You ordained my days
before I was born, and You did not plan for me
to fail, but You positioned me to be more
than a conqueror in Christ.

Heavenly Father,
You are my healer and my hope.
Please help me to stop sabotaging myself, and
give me supernatural strategies to stand
against every ploy of the adversary.

Thank You for helping me to live in Your power.
May all that I do bring You glory.
In Jesus' name

*My dear children, you belong to God
and have defeated them; because God's
Spirit, who is in you, is greater than
the devil, who is in the world.
1 John 4:4 NCV*

*But the Lord is faithful;
he will make you strong and guard you
from satanic attacks of every kind.
2 Thessalonians 3:3 TLB*

42

The Battle Is Real

The devil is not a myth, and his works are not just some scary scene you see on a horror show. The devil is real, and he does not work alone. There is a host of mighty powers that continuously work against our good. Ephesians 6:12 NLT says, "We are not fighting against flesh-and-blood enemies, but against evil rulers and authorities of the unseen world, against mighty powers in this dark world, and against evil spirits in the heavenly places," and in 1 Peter 5:8 NLT it says, "Stay alert! Watch out for your great enemy, the devil. He prowls around like a roaring lion, looking for someone to devour."

The devil does not care about your desire to do right. Your efforts are meaningless to him. His strategy is to distract you, hoping you will stumble and fall under the weight of temptation. So, if overeating is a weak area for you, expect visions of sugary treats to tempt you late at night and other random thoughts to pop in your head enticing you to eat. Do not be surprised when you find yourself eating without concern for your health, appeasing your emotions with food, or feeling discouraged because you struggle to do what is best for your body. The devil focuses on our weaknesses, and while we cannot blame him for everything we do wrong, the more we yield to temptation, the easier it is for the enemy to trap us.

Wake up and stay alert to the works of darkness. The battle is real, and your enemy is relentless. "Submit to God. Resist the devil [stand firm against him] and he will flee from you" (James 4:7 AMP).

Submit to [the authority of] God. Resist the devil
[stand firm against him] and he will flee from you.
James 4:7 AMP

Prophetic Affirmations

I submit to the authority of God
I resist the devil
I stand firm against the enemy
The devil will flee from me

I submit to the authority of God
I resist the devil
I stand firm against the enemy
The devil will flee from me

The scriptures are the inspired Word of God.
Speak them often and empower yourself with truth.

I submit to the authority of God
I resist the devil
I stand firm against the enemy
The devil will flee from me

Prayer for Today

Most Holy Lord,
You reign over the heavens and the earth.
You alone possess all power and might.

Please help me to stay alert
to the strategies of the devil.

Please help me to stand in Your power
so that I will not give the works
of darkness a foothold in my life.

Most Holy Lord,
I submit to Your authority.
Thank You for giving me the victory.
In Jesus' name, I pray

When the people saw that Moses delayed coming
down from the mountain, they gathered around Aaron.
They said to him…"Make gods who will lead us."
Aaron said to them, "Have your wives, sons, and
daughters take off the gold earrings they are wearing,
and bring them to me." So all the people took off
their gold earrings and handed them to Aaron.
After he had worked on the gold with a tool,
he made it into a statue of a calf. Then they
said, "Israel, here are your gods …"
Exodus 32:1-4 GW

The heart is hopelessly dark and deceitful,
a puzzle that no one can figure out. But I, God,
search the heart and examine the mind. I get to the
heart of the human. I get to the root of things. I treat
them as they really are, not as they pretend to be.
Jeremiah 17:9-10 MSG

43

The Inner You

On my way to church one Sunday, I had a desire to stop at the store and buy some goodies to eat. As I thought about stopping, I also paused to ask myself, "Why the urge to eat junk food"? The reply came to me surprisingly quick. "Because I can" were the words I heard in my spirit. I pondered on that statement the entire day. The words, echoing in my head, seemed so detrimental, almost frightening. The tone of my inward voice was sure, clearly demonstrating a spirit of unrestrained behavior and spoke volumes as to what was in my heart.

I wondered if that was how the children of Israel felt when they decided to make a calf from pieces of gold and worship it. Surely, they must have known that a calf made of metal could not profit them, but they chose to do what they wanted. They took their eyes off God, lost focus of who they were, and begin to do things just because they could.

We can do whatever we want because God gave us a free will. We can choose to eat right and promote our health, or we can choose to eat whatever comes our way and harm our bodies. It is our choice.

We may not know the deep-rooted issues for why we do things that devalue our lives and draw us away from our God-given purpose. But our heavenly Father knows the motives of our hearts, and He will give us the insight we need. The answer may come through prayer, another person, the scriptures, or self-reflection. The important thing is to learn about ourselves, grow in the knowledge of God, and live the abundant life He created us to live.

You say, "I am allowed to do anything"—but not everything is good for you. You say, "I am allowed to do anything"—but not everything is beneficial. You could say, "Anything goes." But the point is not to just get by. We want to live well.
1 Corinthians 10:23 MSG, NLT

Prophetic Affirmations

I will live well
I will do what is beneficial for my body
I will do what is best for my health

Speak the words again.
Renew your thoughts by what you hear.

I will live well
I will do what is beneficial for my body
I will do what is best for my health

Speak the words again.
Improve your life by what you say.

I will live well
I will do what is beneficial for my body
I will do what is best for my health

Prayer for Today

Glorious God, Father of all Grace,
Your ways are higher than mine, and Your
thoughts far exceed my understanding.
You know everything about me.
There is nothing hidden from You.

Forgive me for the times I have
diverted off course and gave in to
my desires just because I could.
Please deliver me from wrong thinking
and help me to honor You with my life.

Thank You for Your grace and for blessing
me with a resolve to eat healthier.
In Jesus' name, I pray

Mark out a straight path for your feet;
stay on the safe path. Don't get sidetracked;
keep your feet from following evil.
Proverbs 4:26-27 NLT

I have stayed on his path and did not turn
from it. I have not left his commands behind.
I have treasured his words in my heart.
Job 23:11-12 GW

44

The Path of Success

Have you considered that every time you ate until you could not see straight, or repeatedly made poor food choices, you were living those moments outside of God's will for your life and positioning yourself for a curse instead of a blessing?

We cannot please God and do whatever we want with our bodies. Overeating, mindless eating, emotional eating…we can call it what we want, but eating without counting the cost makes us weak and susceptible to all kinds of conditions and illnesses. It also makes us vulnerable to temptation and easy prey for the devil. More importantly, when we abandon our health for the sake of food, we dishonor God, and we dishonor our lives.

The almighty, self-existing God, who made the earth by His power and rules the universe by His command, desires that we prosper in all things and glorify Him in whatever we do.

Every day you have to choose whether you will live your life according to God's will, or the whims of your flesh. You have to decide if you will honor the body God gave you or tear it down through mindless eating. You have to choose whether you will live with purpose and intent or meander through life lusting after food.

Position yourself for a blessing. Make plans, set goals, and get a vision of where you want to go. Trust God and be prayerful above all else. Celebrate your victories one day at a time and stay on the path of success until eating healthy is no longer a struggle, but a way of life.

Make sure you are going the right way,
and nothing will make you fall.
Proverbs 4:26 ERV

Prophetic Affirmations

I am going the right way
Nothing will make me fall
I will succeed
I will do what is best for my body

Speak the words over and over.
Use your voice to empower yourself.

I am going the right way
Nothing will make me fall
I will succeed
I will do what is best for my body

I am going the right way
Nothing will make me fall
I will succeed
I will do what is best for my body

Prayer for Today

Faithful and True God,
Your mercies never fail and Your
goodness is everlasting.

No matter how many times I stumble,
You are there helping me with my struggles
and giving me the strength to do what is right.

Thank You for caring about me
and for helping me to care about myself.
You are a gracious God.
You are a holy God.
You are worthy of the highest praise.
I am forever grateful to You.
In Jesus' name

Lord, remind me how brief my time on earth will be. Remind me that my days are numbered—how fleeting my life is. You have made my life no longer than the width of my hand. My entire lifetime is just a moment to you at best, each of us is but a breath.
Psalm 39:4-5 NLT

45

Today Is Tomorrow

Today is the tomorrow I put on the calendar as a more suitable time to change my ways. Today is the tomorrow I reasoned in my mind as a better day to relinquish my eating habits to God. Today is the tomorrow that I said would be a good time to stop eating mindlessly, and today is the tomorrow that I vowed to myself I would wake up, take care of my body, and eat as I should.

Now tomorrow is here, but my resolve is weak. I have made so many excuses to indulge in food that I find myself looking for another reason to keep eating. I know I can change. I know I can eat healthier. But when will I do it? When will I stop making excuses? When will I love myself enough to do what is best for my body?

Maybe you struggle with putting off for tomorrow what you could do today. Perhaps you have made countless excuses to justify your eating habits. And maybe, like myself, you are stuck in the snare of procrastination and lack the commitment to do what it takes to change the way you eat.

We do not know the length of our days, or how long we can avoid sickness and disease, brought on by bad eating habits. What we do know, according to James 4:14 NLT, is that our life "is like the morning fog—it's here a little while, then it's gone."

I encourage you to be mindful of the times and to do what you know to do today. Live your life with intent and purpose. Live it well, and let every day be the day that you do what is best for your health.

So be careful how you live; be mindful of your steps.
Don't run around like idiots as the rest of the world does.
Instead, walk as the wise! Make the most of every living
and breathing moment because these are evil times.
Ephesians 5:15-16 VOICE

Prophetic Affirmations

I am careful how I live
I am mindful of my steps
I make the most of every breathing moment

I am careful how I live
I am mindful of my steps
I make the most of every breathing moment

Over and over speak these words.
Morning and night remind yourself that today
is the day to do what you know you should.

I am careful how I live
I am mindful of my steps
I make the most of every breathing moment

Prayer for Today

Heavenly Father,
I pray to You because You are God.
I pray to You because You are my Lord.

Please forgive me for the countless excuses
I have made so I could eat what I wanted,
instead of eating what was good for me.

I have spoken the affirmations, but I know it
takes more than words to achieve victory.
Please help me to do what I say.

Thank You for giving me the grace to succeed.
In Jesus' name

The words of a person's mouth are
like deep waters. The fountain of wisdom
is an overflowing stream.
Proverbs 18:4 GW

Wise words satisfy like a good meal;
the right words bring satisfaction.
Proverbs 18:20 NLT

46

Use Your Voice

"I will always be like this. I will not make it. I cannot do it. Who cares how I look? I should give up." These are words of defeat that invade our thoughts, taunting, tormenting, and tempting us to give in to our struggles and walk away from our intended purpose.

We can allow these destructive thoughts to fester, dictate our actions, and interfere with our God-given destiny, or we can counteract them by using our voice to speak words that give us hope and help us to achieve victory in every area of life.

Remind yourself often that God predestined you for good works and He walks alongside you to fulfill your purpose. Say out loud, that God gave you a spirit of self-control, and you can do what is best for your body. Rehearse the fact that God desires that you prosper in all things, even in your health. Read scriptures on the promises and plans of God. Then speak about His eternal power, His unwavering strength that He gives to the weak, and His faithfulness to help us endure. Over and over affirm yourself with truth, regardless of how many times you stumble. Fight your thoughts with the Word of God. Win the battle in your mind by what you say.

Take time to quiet yourself and listen carefully to your internal dialogue. Whatever negative thoughts are going on in your head, use your voice to counteract them. Use your voice to express words that encourage, equip, and empower you. Use your voice to create new beliefs. Use your voice to change your life.

Death and life are in the power of the tongue.
Proverbs 18:21 NKJV

Prophetic Affirmations

I speak words of life
I speak words that give me hope
I speak words that bring me peace
I speak words that encourage my soul
I speak words to empower myself
I speak words to create a change in my life

Use your voice to fight your thoughts.
Win the battle in your mind by what you say.

I speak words of life
I speak words that give me hope
I speak words that bring me peace
I speak words that encourage my soul
I speak words to empower myself
I speak words to create a change in my life

Prayer for Today

Heavenly Father,
You are the only living God,
and Your Word is alive and full of power.

Forgive me for the times I chose to stuff my mouth
with food instead of using my voice to speak.

Please help me to meditate on Your Word,
to speak Your Word, and to live by Your Word.

May I honor You in all that I do.
In Jesus' name

You're blessed when you stay on course,
walking steadily on the road revealed by God.
You're blessed when you follow his
directions, doing your best to find him. That's
right— you don't go off on your own; you
walk straight along the road he set.
Psalm 119:1-3 MSG

47

Watch Your Walk

Some years ago, a few co-workers and I were sharing our particular shortcomings. Two women shared how they wanted to quit smoking cigarettes, another had a drinking problem, and I needed to stop eating junk food. We had heartfelt testimony, empathized with each other, had a time of prayer, and went our separate ways. The women with the smoking problem immediately went downstairs to smoke cigarettes, and I helped myself to the contents of someone's candy jar before I even reached my desk.

I felt perplexed in my spirit as I watched us do the very things we had just shared. Without hesitation, I asked the Lord, "Why did we do that?" God spoke quickly and quietly to my heart and said, "Because you walk amiss." We were walking in a wrong and imperfect way and dominated by unrestrained behavior.

In hindsight, we had shared and prayed about our struggles, but we had not discussed ways to overcome them. With that said, I encourage you to do more than identify your weaknesses. Forgive yourself for abusing your body and envision a future without addictions and harmful habits. Then make a plan to live a healthier life, tie it to a goal, and commit wholeheartedly to the process.

You are not alone on your journey. The Almighty God is always with you. Just remember to "Keep your eyes on [His] path and look straight ahead. Make sure you are going the right way, and nothing will make you fall" (Proverbs 4:25-26 ERV).

*Don't veer off to the right or the left. Walk
straight down the road God commands so that
you'll have a good life and live a long time.*
Deuteronomy 5:33 MSG

*Let me see your kindness to me in the
morning, for I am trusting you. Show me
where to walk, for my prayer is sincere.*
Psalm 143:8 TLB

Prophetic Affirmations

I am trusting God
God is showing me where to walk
I am looking straight ahead
I am walking in a right way

Keep talking about what you are doing.
Keep talking until you do what you say.

I am trusting God
God is showing me where to walk
I am looking straight ahead
I am walking in a right way

Prayer for Today

Merciful God,
You give strength to the weak.
You are the Lord who forgives.
You are worthy to be praised.

Forgive me for walking in a wrong way.
Forgive me for eating mindlessly.
Please help me to stay on the right path
and to live a healthier life.

Nothing is worth being out of Your will.
Nothing is worth jeopardizing my health.

Please help me to do things Your way.
In Jesus' name

And we are confident that he hears us whenever we ask for anything that pleases him. And since we know he hears us when we make our requests, we also know that he will give us what we ask for.
1 John 5:14-15 NLT

Look deep into my heart, God, and find out everything I am thinking.
Psalm 139:23 CEV

48

What Are You Thinking?

One day a pastor friend of mine gave me a message from God, which was to ask Him what my eating struggle was masking. In obedience, I asked God the question, and a few days later as I was standing in a room with several vending machines at my disposal, this thought popped in my head, "Only people who do not know who they are have to eat candy." I immediately said to myself, "I know who I am. I am a child of God, and I do not have to eat candy."

A few days later, as I was walking down the chip aisle in the grocery store, this thought arose: "Only failures and gullible people eat chips." Oh, my goodness! Where did that come from, I thought, because I have never thought of myself as gullible or a failure. But, God, who knows our deepest thoughts, was showing me that was exactly what I felt about myself when I chose to eat junk food.

Both situations were insightful and worked for my good. The vending machine incident was empowering, and many times since when I see candy on a store shelf, I say, "I know who I am. I am a child of God, and I do not have to eat candy." The grocery store experience revealed feelings of unworthiness I did not know existed. Going forward, I begin to speak words to negate those thoughts and acknowledged that the child of God that does not have to eat candy is the same child of God who is a neither gullible nor a failure.

I encourage you to ask God to tell you what your eating struggle is masking. Ask God to show you what you think about yourself.

His unchanging plan has always been to
adopt us into his own family by sending Jesus Christ
to die for us. And he did this because he wanted to!
Ephesians 1:5 TLB

Prophetic Affirmations

I am a child of God
I belong to the family of God
I belong to the creator of the world
I belong to Jesus

Keep speaking until you believe what you say.

I am a child of God
I belong to the family of God
I belong to the creator of the world
I belong to Jesus

I am a child of God
I belong to the family of God
I belong to the creator of the world
I belong to Jesus

Prayer for Today

Dear Lord,
You are a great God who knows all things.
Please show me what my eating struggle is masking.
Reveal to me things I cannot find out on my own.
Open my eyes so I can see the hidden things.
Open my eyes so I can see myself as You see me.
In Jesus' name, I pray

But you must remain strong
and not become discouraged.
Your actions will be rewarded.
2 Chronicles 15:7 GW

For nothing will be impossible with God.
Luke 1:37 ERV

49

Words of Life

The day did come when See's Candy did little for my palate, and the cookies I had savored for years no longer called my name. The season did arrive when donuts felt like grease and sugar coursing through my body and overrode my desire to indulge. It did happen. I defeated the junk food bandit. The thief who came to take my life, breaking me down through unrestrained eating, weight gain, and all kinds of physical discomforts, no longer had control over me. I triumphed over gluttony and stood my ground against mindless eating. The day did come, but it did not happen without stumbling and falling, and certainly not without trusting and obeying God.

I did what God said, which was to affirm myself with truth from the scriptures. It took a while, and not because speaking affirmations is ineffectual, but because I chose not to speak. Now while that sounds incredulous, the reality for many of us is that we put off doing what we know we should so that we can keep doing what we want, even when we know that procrastination is self-defeating and gets us nowhere.

Do not get me wrong for I still enjoy a treat or two, but eating without counting the cost is a risk I am not willing to take. No amount of food is worth my health, and nothing tastes better than obeying God and living out the purpose He ordained for me.

I urge you, with every fiber of my being, to affirm yourself with words that align with the scriptures, words that give you hope, and words that empower you to triumph in every aspect of life.

Words kill, words give life; they're either
poison or fruit—you choose.
Proverbs 18:21 MSG

Prophetic Affirmations

I affirm myself with truth
I affirm myself with words that agree with God
I affirm myself with words of life
I affirm myself with words of power

Increase your faith by the words you speak.

I affirm myself with truth
I affirm myself with words that agree with God
I affirm myself with words of life
I affirm myself with words of power

Change your life by what you say.

I affirm myself with truth
I affirm myself with words that agree with God
I affirm myself with words of life
I affirm myself with words of power

Prayer for Today

Most Gracious God,
Your words are powerful and effective.
Your words never fail to give me hope.
Your words never fail to strengthen me.
Your words are alive and active.
Your words are righteous and true.

Most Gracious God,
Thank You for helping me to speak words of life.
Thank You for helping me to change the way I eat.
In Jesus' name

God—you're my God. I can't get enough of you!
I've worked up such hunger and thirst for God,
traveling across dry and weary deserts. So here
I am in the place of worship, eyes open,
drinking in your strength and glory. In your
generous love I am really living at last! My lips
brim praises like fountains. I bless you every time
I take a breath; my arms wave like
banners of praise to you.
Psalm 63:1-4 MSG

50

Your Best Life

No matter what your day holds, communicating with God first is the wisest thing you can do. For who can better lead you in the right way than the one who created you and knows what is best for your life. On the contrary, if you consistently make God an afterthought and yield to the demands of your day instead, you will become spiritually weak and distracted by worldly pursuits and the conditions of life. You will also be unaware of the strategies the devil has set up against you.

Your days may go well, and your life may be good, but you will never live your best life apart from God, who is sovereign over all things. You cannot accomplish God's will without His wisdom, nor walk a righteous path without His direction. You certainly cannot work through your weaknesses without the Lord's strength.

The more you acknowledge God in everyday things, the more He will show up in every aspect of your life. Romans 12:1 MSG says, "Take your everyday, ordinary life, your sleeping, eating, going-to-work, and walking-around life-and place it before God as an offering." When you do this, God will bless you with everything you need to live the life He planned for you. Not a life devoid of struggles, but a life where you will experience hope, purpose, and victory.

God did not create us to live our lives apart from Him, but He did give us a free will. Therefore, choose God and receive a multitude of blessings. Your heavenly Father will equip you and empower you to not only live a good life but your best life.

Seek the Kingdom of God above all else,
and live righteously, and he will
give you everything you need.
Matthew 6:33 NLT

Prophetic Affirmations

I seek God above all else
I choose to live righteously
God gives me everything I need

Keep speaking. Bless your life by what you say!

I seek God above all else
I choose to live righteously
God gives me everything I need

I seek God above all else
I choose to live righteously
God gives me everything I need

Prayer for Today

Holy God,
You are the First and the Last,
the Alpha and the Omega,
the Beginning and the End.

Forgive me for the times
that I did not acknowledge You.
Forgive me for not seeking You first.

Holy God,
I choose You, Lord.
I choose to live my best life now.
I choose to do things Your way.
In Jesus' name, I pray

Your words are what sustain me;
they are food to my hungry soul.
Jeremiah 15:16 TLB

All kinds of food delight our palates and satisfy
our stomachs, but there is nothing that tastes better than
the goodness of God, nor is sweeter than the Holy Spirit's
presence. There is nothing that can feed you like His
faithfulness nor sustain you like His Word.

Eat to live, and live well, but savor all that God
has to give, for in Him you will never hunger and
in Him, you will never thirst.

Printed in the United States
by Baker & Taylor Publisher Services